CREATIVE WORK

THE CONSTRUCTIVE ROLE OF BUSINESS IN A TRANSFORMING SOCIETY

CREATIVE WORK

THE CONSTRUCTIVE ROLE OF BUSINESS IN A TRANSFORMING SOCIETY

WILLIS HARMAN
JOHN HORMANN

AFTERWORD BY
STAN JANGER AND AMY EDMONDSON

A Study for the Schweisfurth Foundation
Munich, Germany

An Institute of Noetic Sciences Publication

 Knowledge Systems, Inc.
Developing Resources for Creative Change

Published by Knowledge Systems, Inc.

For a free catalog or ordering information
call (317) 241-0749 or write Knowledge Systems,
7777 West Morris Street, Indianapolis, IN 46231.

Library of Congress Cataloging-in-Publication Data
Harman, Willis W.
    Creative work: the constructive role of business in transforming society / Willis Harman, John Hormann ; afterword by Stan Janger and Amy Edmondson.
        p.   cm.
    "An Institute of Noetic Sciences publication.
    "A study for the Schweisfurth Foundation, Munich, Germany."
    Includes bibliographical references and index.
    ISBN 0-941705-11-0 : $18.95. -- ISBN 0-941705-12-9 (pbk.) : $12.95
    1. Industry--Social aspects.   2. Creative ability in business.
3. Organizational effectiveness.   I. Hormann, John, 1934-   .
II. Institute of Noetic Sciences. III. Schweisfurth Foundation (Munich, Germany) IV. Title.
    HD60.H38 1990
    306.3--dc20
                                                            90-44481
                                                            CIP

10 9 8 7 6 5 4 3 2 1

Dedicated to those who are
searching for new and liberating horizons
and are prepared to go beyond fear and hope

Contents

Preface 1

A friend recently gave me a copy of Dominique Lapierre's novel *The City of Joy*. The book is about altruism and love; it is one of the most moving and inspiring books I have ever read. It is, in part, the story of a Polish priest, Stephan Kovalski, who comes to Calcutta to help, and voluntarily to share living conditions with, the poorest of the poor. One cannot but be deeply moved by this tale of loving sacrifice. But what struck me most was the realization that these displaced peasants were forced to leave their lands in West Bengal and elsewhere, to crowd into a Calcutta slum under utterly miserable conditions, because of a combination of factors over which they had no control. Some of these factors were called "progress" from the vantage point of more fortunate persons; others were the inexorable grinding of a malfunctioning social system; others were natural disasters. It is noble of Kovalski and countless others like him to help the starving poor; would it not be at least as noble to work to eliminate the conditions that *generated* the poor, the underemployed, the shameful waste of human lives? Whereas we can readily see what one might do to help the starving poor, we are intimidated by the concept of changing a whole socio-political-economic system, because one hardly knows where to start.

One group that has set out to do something about the problem of world hunger is "The Hunger Project." I believe that the basic concept underlying this effort is totally sound: The first step in eliminating hunger on the planet is to change our belief that hunger is tolerable. Once that happens, there appear a multitude of ways in which the efforts of individuals can contribute. I have both respect and admiration for the tens of thousands of persons actively involved in this Project; it is a wonderful thing that so many are now attempting to help. However, when one looks deeply into the origins of chronic hunger, it has to do with deep-rooted system characteristics. It is noble to enlist in such a bold attempt to cure hunger. Is it less noble to ask what kinds of whole-system change might make it more possible for persons to lead productive lives?

The United States has increasingly severe problems of the aging and the homeless. Through conditions beyond their control, many of the aging lack adequate housing and health care. Perhaps government will mount programs to provide homes, shelters, and medical services. But that does not solve the problem at the most fundamental level. What characteristics of the system cause it to generate indigent aged and homeless people? And how can those characteristics be changed?

Most fundamentally, what evolutionary system change would increase the likelihood that practically everyone has the opportunity to be engaged in dignified and satisfying work, and has full guarantee of satisfaction of his or her basic human needs?

These are the questions we set out to address. We believe that they are questions all too often not asked, because the temptation is great to attack the symptoms rather than attempt to create change at a more fundamental level.

Whether or not we have succeeded in producing a useful analysis must be judged by the reader. I can say for myself that working on this research with John Hormann has been one of the most rewarding activities of my life. Furthermore, I am totally convinced of the extreme importance of the inquiry.

We wish to acknowledge the support of the Schweisfurth Foundation and the Institute of Noetic Sciences. Many individuals contributed their insight to this report, through commenting on early drafts, through contributing to the research effort, and in stimulating conversations. Among these, we want to mention especially the generous time and effort by Herman Maynard, Susan Mehrtens, and JoAnn McAllister. Stan Janger and Amy Edmondson contributed a valuable Afterword, which provides examples of "new paradigm thinking" in action.

Willis W. Harman
Sausalito, California
June 1990

Preface 2

Those who search for understanding and truth encounter uncertainty. To cope with the discomfort of this uncertainty, we come to *believe*; and the belief-and-value systems we adopt offer hope. But this hope lures our awareness into contemplating a "better" future, and raises our expectations. As a result, our tasks in the NOW are performed with only partial attention.

In the depth of our consciousness we know that the future evolves out of the quality of today's thoughts, feelings and actions. Out of this knowledge is born the fear that our hopes could be deceptive. That fear influences further developments. Expectation creates its opposing force; the pendulum dynamic between hope and fear has its beginning.

This insecurity drives us to value judgments; we divide the world into "good" and "bad," and identify with the "good." This split identification gives us a temporary feeling of security, but again the division produces its opposing force and deforms our relation to reality. Problems are detached from their context, dealt with in isolation, and reappear in other forms—as new problems, disillusionments, or constraints.

In this dilemma we continually try to shape people and our environment to fit our concepts and values. By doing so we block out the richness and variety of life; our lives are impoverished. Even the search for life purpose cannot fill this void in the long run, and results in a craving for prestige, power, "love," and security.

Our search for security leads us to strive for perfection. Striving for perfection develops its own dynamic and complexity, making life seem more intricate and difficult. Finally, we abdicate our own responsibility and surrender our integrity, arriving at our present situation: "authorities" who claim to know what is "right" and "wrong," tightly holding on to their false concepts, endangering life on the planet. Weapons that can destroy us a thousand-fold are placed around the world to "secure peace." Agricultural industry and the noxious fumes of traffic poison our food, air, and water. All of this is supposedly "progress"; it contributes to "national security" and to the GNP. Education, art, nursery schools, health programs, and care for the aged are "cost factors."

Business has carved economics out of ecology. It tends to monetize human values and to lack a higher purpose. Applying economic logic, it makes decisions that deeply influence future generations on the basis of the next quarterly financial report. There are some in the upper levels of business management who, however affluent personally, and in positions of apparent power, nevertheless appear to have a poverty-stricken mind-set in that they exhibit a persistent fear of not having enough.

Addiction to prestige and security has transferred the conflict into the arena of work. Wherever there is a discrepancy between words and deeds, people turn away, either overtly or through "mental notice of termination." We practice faultseeking, which prevents learning from mistakes and creates employees unwilling to risk. The anxiety and unwillingness to relate to others created by fear of risk undermines the courage required for honesty, trust, communication and creativity. At the end waits the paralyzing identity crisis, leading to indolence and resignation, which cannot be cured by more money or more free time.

However, there are those who have freed themselves from such fear and, finding exhilaration in the challenge of the creative response, are liberated to do strategic thinking in the broadest sense. Open awareness, willingness to see reality as it is, enables us to be authentic. When we learn to trust the intelligence of our whole organism, we can act appropriately in critical situations and do not have to rely on the rational mind only. We can create space in our awareness for the variety of life. We can learn to discern and organize beyond value judgment and so can dissolve mental restrictions. We will recognize far-reaching connections and can choose and decide from this extended view.

From this perspective, work will be more than earning money. Economy will be part of ecology. Business, metaphysics and art will be a unit, which employs the total person creatively in the work process. Nourishment will be more than sustaining the body. Psyche and body will be experienced as the unit they are. The past will be part of the present. Out of this comprehensive view we can shape a future that unfolds new and liberating horizons.

Business, the motor of our society, has the opportunity to be a new creative force on the planet, a force which could contribute to the well-being of many. For that to occur, we must all substantially increase our commitment to integrity and accountability, and courageously make a quantum leap in consciousness: *beyond conventional solutions; beyond opposing forces; beyond fear and hope.*

This book is for those who cherish such a vision.

John V. Hormann
Munich, Germany
June 1990

Introduction

A change appears to be underway throughout the industrialized world which involves reassessment of the most basic assumptions underlying Western society, its technological infrastructure and the world economy. In plainer terms, we seem to be in a transition of a magnitude comparable with the Industrial Revolution or the discovery that the Earth is not flat, but global.

Whether or not it is possible to arrive at a consensus as to the detailed description of that change, we can feel fairly certain that the next couple of decades will be a period of fundamental transition, through rough and uncharted waters.

To continue with the maritime metaphor, as there is no accurate chart of the future, long-range navigation is a futile exercise. What we need most, then, is (a) as good a sensing as we can get, both of society's destination and of the perils along the way, and (b) accurate soundings as we proceed.

Each of us in our daily lives, with every action decision we take, tacitly assumes some interpretation of our situation—some chart, as it were, of society's probable course into the future. The best available navigation chart contains rumors of a New World out to the West, reported sightings of a number of rocks and shoals, and lots of *terra incognita*. The important thing is to have that chart contain the best information available at the moment, and at the same time to be totally open to new sightings or soundings which might indicate a need to alter the anticipated course. No interpretation is demonstrably the "correct" one; each day's further movement through the passage to the future provides new data that either fits with our tentative chart or forces us to consider a modification. Whatever chart one is influenced by, that sort of open-minded testing is essential.

There are many points from which one might set out to construct this sort of mapping of possible paths to the future. For a variety of reasons that will become more clear, we have chosen to center the present exploration around *the role of work*, both in the lives of individuals and in society. But, if work is assumed to be a key feature of our journey into the future, many other interrelated facets must be viewed simultaneously to obtain an adequate comprehension of the whole.

First, there are the problems—global environmental deterioration; the possibility of irreversible, man-made climate change; the extinction at an alarming rate of more and more species of plants and animals; deforestation and desertification; growing scarcity of fresh water; accumulations of toxic chemicals; chronic poverty and hunger in large portions of the world; persistent social problems of crime, terrorism, and drug addiction; the instability of the debt-ridden world economy; and, of course, the ever-present threat of international conflict with use of nuclear weapons. The list seems to be endless, and all of the problems are interrelated so that measures taken to ameliorate any one of them sends reverberations throughout the whole system. A diversity of social and political movements comprise a second part of the picture—movements promoting democracy, liberation, ecological awareness, feminine consciousness, world peace, social justice. And thirdly, at a still deeper level in the structure of society we can find indications of a revolutionary shift in the most basic assumptions about the nature of reality—assumptions that underlie modern society and all its institutions.

The primary investigators in this project have been watching these highly interconnected developments for some years and have been struck by the fact that reassessing the role of work, which seems so central to the ultimate resolution of our dilemmas, is so little talked about. The possibility that the world economy will not be able in the future to provide anything like full employment, as that term has been conventionally understood, is such a threatening idea that the topic almost seems to be taboo. Reports that many workers in the modern economy are alienated and find their work meaningless are also threatening in their implications. Furthermore, those who discuss the economics of work seldom deal adequately with issues of meaning, and those who are concerned with the ways people seek to discover the meaning of life seldom appear competent to deal with the economics of work.

If there has been a reluctance to face certain aspects of the work issue, it is no doubt partly because the problems appear to be so intractable. And indeed they are, if one assumes that they must somehow be solved through actions by governments or through top-down management. So many things have been tried—from job-creation and vocational education programs to more thoroughgoing changes such as the welfare state and the centrally planned communist state—and there have been so many disappointments!

And yet there is another possibility, which, when it is viewed in the light of recent developments in Eastern Europe, China, and other parts of the world, seems far more plausible than would have been the case a decade ago. That is the possibility that the dilemmas are resolvable through a still more fundamental transformation of modern industrial society—a transformation which could come about, not through clever management from a powerful state or transnational institution, but through a bubbling up of new goals, values, commitments, and concepts, coming from a *vast, creative middle band* of people who sense a new vision and will be satisfied with nothing short of its realization. It is a "middle band" because it tends not to include the two extremes—those who are very successful (although perhaps unfulfilled) playing by the old rules, and those people who are left marginal and powerless by the old rules.

The revolutions of Eastern Europe are incomplete; people are very clear about what they *don't* want, but far less than explicit about what they do want. We in the modern capitalist countries are in a similar situation. It is rapidly becoming clear what is not working; we have yet to form a vision of the global society that does work.

Somewhat as the people of Eastern Europe, in the latter part of the 1980s, awakened to their power to bring about increased liberty and democracy, so it may be—and our research would so suggest—that another awakening is underway in the Western countries. This is an awakening to the power to bring about a society in which such concepts as unemployment and "meaningless" labor are obsolete, a society in which everyone has the opportunity to be engaged in dignified and satisfying work. This awakening is not being led by some charismatic leaders, political or otherwise; rather, it is arising in what appears to be a spontaneous manner, out of the deeper values and intuition of hundreds of thousands of people. It might be interpreted as evidence that modern society is in the process of healing itself.

Self-healing forces in society. Living organisms are self-healing to a considerable extent. The same can undoubtedly be said of societies even though the mechanisms are less studied. The Gaia hypothesis, which has recently been attracting much favorable attention, suggests that the planet, as a living system, may be self-healing as well. Of course, there is no assurance that the healing process of the planet guarantees the continued existence of human civilization; humans will have to see to that themselves.

As we approached this research, our preliminary understandings seemed to support one assumption: Whereas there is undoubtedly a great deal of denial with regard to recognizing the true depth and seriousness of present societal and global problems, there appear at the same time many indications of a spontaneous creative response. These include the social movements already referred to, as well as a host of innovative experiments in nonprofit organizations, intentional communities, alternative economies, alternative health-care programs, new forms of business entrepreneurship, citizen approaches to assisting new enterprise and community development in Third World countries, and many others. Rather than choosing a conservative skepticism with regard to all of this, we elected to explore the optimistic hypothesis that much of what we see going on around us can be interpreted as self-healing impulses, partially unconsciously guided.

Thus with this research we attempt to explore the hypothesis that (a) whole-system change will be required for the major societal and global problems to become solvable; (b) at some deep intuitive level people seem to sense this, and as a result spontaneous social movements and experiments have arisen which, taken together, provide both direction and motive force for such whole-system change; and (c) as the dynamics of this process of social transformation are better understood, actions that foster constructive change can be supported to help minimize the social disruption and human misery that have so often in the past accompanied deep social change.

This is all of the greatest significance to business. In the first place, making good corporate decisions depends critically on accurate assessment of both the external and the internal environment. But also, and most importantly, business leadership is in a unique position from which to contribute constructively to peaceful transformation.

It is both typical and reasonable for the business executive to want to know: What should I do? By the very nature of the situation, the most creative response is not likely to be a specific action, but rather more like a different stance, a new way of viewing, a changed basis for choices.

In the final chapter we do try to respond to this perfectly valid question, with a three-part answer:

1. Come to understand the nature of the transformational forces present in the modern world so as to increase your organization's chances of survival through what is likely to be a chaotic transition period.

2. Do what is necessary to prosper, in the sense of being strong and flourishing, because that strength will be needed to make an effective contribution to the evolution of the whole. One of the most important factors here is attracting and holding the most creative and competent people.
3. Contribute, because only if everybody does are we likely to see a successful outcome following this very critical time.

Of course, we have some rather specific suggestions under each of these three headings, as well as some cautions about what are reasonable expectations.

Outline of the report. Having done the research and come up with what we believe are important insights, how do we tell the story? An essay seemed to be the best form—one not laden with the niceties of academic presentation, yet including enough evidence so the conclusions would be plausible. We would have liked it to be simple and brief. Yet some of the concepts require deep thought; superficial consideration and neat action plans won't do. We have told it as briefly as we felt able.

The report begins with an initial chapter summarizing the work dilemma and its possible resolution. In Chapter 2 we analyze the manifest problems and dilemmas, emphasizing the ways in which they seem so intractable, and search for their origins in the development and basic characteristics of modern society. Chapter 3 analyzes the major social and political movements of our day, with particular emphasis on the directions of change which they signal as desirable. In Chapter 4 we combine the outcomes of these two analyses in order to test our hypothesis that *the movements for personal and social transformation which have developed spontaneously over the last 30 years contain within them the elements of successful resolution of our most vexing dilemmas.* Chapter 5 looks into the dynamic processes of social change, and inquires into the conditions for fundamental societal change that is not socially disruptive. Finally, Chapter 6 investigates the features of the emerging society and addresses the important challenges to the business community to play a constructive part in redefining and reshaping the world of work for the benefit of the global community and, indeed, for the Earth itself.

One caveat is necessary. The most serious problems society faces are essentially global. Furthermore, we argue below that some sort of global system change will be required for the satisfactory resolution of the problems. However, our analysis is mainly from the viewpoint of the dominant societies in Western Europe and North America. We justify this primarily on the basis of the pervasiveness of the influence of modern, Western industrial society on the rest of the globe and the power the West exerts politically to satisfy its own demands. We make no pretense of dealing with the special problems of Japan, say, or the Soviet Union, or South Africa. Nonetheless, we would hope that our analysis could be a valuable input to similar analyses for those other areas. Similarly we do not deal explicitly with the situations in specific developing countries; we do, however, consider the development dilemma as a world problem.

To begin then, let us address why there is a fundamental work dilemma, why it is resolvable, and what sort of change will be required for its satisfactory resolution.

Chapter 1

The Changing Nature of Work

Without work, all life goes rotten—but
when work is soulless, life stifles and dies.
ALBERT CAMUS

There may be no aspect of the future about which modern society is more confused than the role of work in the life of the individual and in society. A basic cause of this confusion is the failure to recognize the full implications of the technological changes that have been taking place. Present conceptions regarding work were formed in an era when the primary societal function of work was the production of necessary or desired goods and services, and in which one could foresee no end to the social desirability of utilizing technological advance to increase the economic productivity of the individual laborer. Yet today those assumptions lead to a fundamental dilemma. On the one hand, if a country does not continually increase labor productivity, the industry of that country tends to become noncompetitive in the international market. On the other hand, if productivity does increase, then by definition, to maintain the same number of jobs the economic product must increase. Thus as various constraints—resource, environmental, political, and social—tend to limit economic growth, *chronic unemployment becomes an intrinsic characteristic of the future*. Since that is an unpleasant thought to contemplate, countries and individuals have tended to use tortuous logic and subtly evasive actions to avoid confronting it.

In a few countries demographic trends are obscuring this unemployment dilemma for the short term, but the tendency is inexorable in the longer term. Some of the obfuscation is more contrived, as is illustrated by the progressive redefinition, in the United States, of the official unemployment rate corresponding to "full employment." This rate, which some claim represents the unemployment level necessary to maintain low inflation rates, has risen steadily from around 2.5 percent in the 1940s to over 7.5 percent in the late 1980s. A nation can, as did the Soviet Union for many years, insure that there is no unemployment by giving every adult a job whether or not their labors are really needed. But this expedient of "makework" creates a serious morale problem, because no one likes to feel unneeded.

Underemployment, working at less that one's full productive capacity, is the other side of the work dilemma. It is a major source of workplace problems and social malaise. In industrialized countries, underemployment is closely related to the prevailing concept of education. Education is viewed in modern society—whether we openly admit it or not—primarily as preparation for a job in the mainstream economy. As the intelligence and educational levels of a people increase (and that is certainly the trend over the long term), increasing numbers of people are unable to find work that uses the skills and knowledge they were trained in. Discontent and alienation are the result. Education is no longer a sure route to increased status, power, and income. Neither does it insure work that is intrinsically challenging and that offers opportunities for creativity and self-expression. Increasing numbers of well-educated workers have to accept jobs—white-collar as well as blue-collar—that are routine, unstimulating, and stultifying. A significant fraction of the jobs in modern society are neither intrinsically challenging nor obviously related to inspiring social challenges. (Maccoby, 1988)

In the developing societies underemployment is in general not a consequence of "over-education," but of the destruction of traditional ways of rural and village cultural patterns. Cities in the Third World bulge with displaced peasants, able only to scratch out the meanest of livings in the most ignoble occupations. In some of these countries underemployment is the condition of the great majority of the urban population.

An aspect of underemployment is revealed by the old story of two stonecutters who were engaged in similar activities. Asked what they were doing, one answered, "I'm squaring up this piece of stone." The other replied, "I'm building a cathedral." The first may have been underemployed; the second was definitely not. The state of underemployment has not so much to do with what work a person is doing, as with what she perceives she is doing it for. The frontiersman, the old-time craftsman, the farmer blessed with a fine piece of land, the mother sewing clothes at home and caring for an infant, all would have scoffed at the idea that they were underemployed. But once mechanized agriculture is available, raising the same crops with hand tools seems less fulfilling; once a robotized assembly line can mass-produce an item, the meaning of the craft, and the challenge to make the same item by hand, are destroyed.

It is worth noting that the famed British economist John Maynard Keynes had recognized this potential problem of "superfluous people" as far back as 1930, when he warned in his *Essays in Persuasion:*

> If the economic problem [the struggle for subsistence] is solved, mankind will be deprived of its traditional purpose.... Thus for the first time since his creation man will be faced with his real, his permanent problem—how to use his freedom from pressing economic cares.... There is no country and no people, I think, who can look forward to the age of leisure and abundance without a dread.... It is a fearful problem for the ordinary person, with no special talents to occupy himself, especially if he no longer has roots to the soil or in custom or in the beloved conventions of a traditional society.

There is reluctant but growing admission in North America and Northern Europe that despite mass consumption and global arms races and a nonproductive but burgeoning "financial industry," the long-term future of industrial society looks to be characterized by chronic unemployment and underemployment. The reasons are basically two: 1) in the long run, economic growth may not continue to generate enough jobs to accommodate the expanding workforce; and 2) the quality of available jobs may not be compatible with the rising educational levels of the workforce.

So what do you do when the productiveness of the economy has risen to where the needs of society can be met employing only a fraction of the potential workforce? The answer implicitly put forth in modern industrial societies is, create more needs! Become obsessed with consumption, to try to use up the product and keep the machinery running. What do you do when technology has advanced to where anything you can train a human to do, you can train a computer (robot) to do; and furthermore the computer will probably do it better, faster, and cheaper? The accepted answer is to become obsessed with economic growth to create new jobs for humans to do. *These are inappropriate responses arising from an inadequate concept of the role of work; they do not address the real human question.*

It is important to recognize that underemployment in the developed world arises partly because of modern society's successes in terms of the degree and diversity of developed capacity among its citizens. The fraction of the population who demonstrate both initiative and realized intellectual, skill-related, and aesthetic capacities is probably higher than for any other society throughout history. Factors that have contributed to this success include diet and nutrition, education, everyday contact with stimulating knowledge and technologies, extended communication, and availability of diverse, challenging roles for people to play. (Schumacher, 1979; Epilogue) It is ironic that this outstanding success should now appear as a problem, namely the difficulties persons experience in finding niches in the mainstream economy within which to manifest their fullest capabilities.

Why is modern society unable to arrange things so that practically every citizen has ample opportunities for meaningful fulfilling work? That is the fundamental question, underlying all the more obvious aspects of work-related problems from unemployment and underemployment, through chronic inner-city poverty and homeless people, to environmental impacts of economic growth. "Meaningful work" is not necessarily work that is exciting and challenging at every moment; it is enough that it be part of a larger endeavor which is infused with meaning. It is mainly that "larger endeavor" for our modern, mass-consumption society which is lacking.

The authors are convinced that the above question is answerable, as well as the follow-on question: What must be done? In preparing this report we have aspired to contribute to the search for those answers.

Thus we have attempted to assess the changing role of work in a far broader context than is usually considered. Furthermore, we have especially focused on the role of business, since the institutions of business are so dominant in modern society. Our objective is to clarify the nature of the modern dilemma, to highlight a few of the kinds of constructive actions already taking place, and to suggest deliberate actions the business sector could undertake to find and play the most constructive role possible.

Work and Meaning in Modern Society

The problems associated with work and meaning involve much more than concerns about unemployment and demands for "meaningful work." In the next chapter we will explore more thoroughly how the dilemma centering around work and meaning is directly connected to many—almost all—of the other perplexing social and global problems. First we need to recall how it came about.

From agricultural to "information" society. The rise of industrial society has been a fantastic success story. Within only a few centuries, Western Europe and America leapt from the relatively low capability and motivation to manipulate the physical environment that characterizes traditional societies, to a technological capability so high that almost anything one can imagine wanting to do seems possible. The wave of industrialization spread around the planet, affecting in time practically every society on the globe—seducing with its glitter those it did not take over by force.

During those centuries, a central focus on economic production seemed to make sense. Providing new tools, making people's labor count for more, converting more and more of the Earth's resources into economic product, exercising increasing "control" over the natural environment through technology, drawing more and more of people's activities into the monetized economy (both as jobs and as "consumed" services)—all appeared to result in an improved material standard of living, and hence to increased human well-being.

As is well known, a key consequence of the evolving Western industrial paradigm was a dramatic change in work patterns. The production of goods through the new industrial methods, as well as the fraction of persons employed in industrial production, began to rise. Workers moved from the farm to towns and cities, and over a period of less than two centuries the workforce directly involved in agricultural production fell from nearly 90 percent in pre-industrial society to as low as a few percent presently in the most technologically advanced nations.

One might possibly have argued that demand for agricultural products would increase as farm labor productivity rose and prices dropped, thus keeping agricultural employment high. By and large, that did not happen. What happened instead was that the demand for agricultural products saturated; it did not rise spectacularly as production per worker steadily increased, rather there was a major displacement of labor from agriculture to industrial production. With modernizing agricultural machinery and methods, fewer persons were required to work the land, and those displaced persons migrated in droves to the industrial centers to work in factories and offices.

As the labor-replacing possibilities of computer-aided automation of industrial production processes became apparent in the early 1960s, fear of technological disemployment grew in many of the countries of Europe and North America. (The situation was somewhat different in Europe than in North America, because of the 1948-1970 reconstruction boom after the ravages of war, and because the post-war demographic bulge was a little later.) A number of well-publicized analyses warned of the approaching unemployment problem, and another number of analyses argued that the fear was unwarranted. The latter insisted that technological advance would create jobs as fast as automation technology replaced them. Implicit in their arguments was a forecasted high growth in consumption of industrial output.

That did not happen either. What happened instead was that employment in goods-producing industries peaked, as early as the 1950s in some countries, and started down. Demand for goods did not rise to maintain employment in industrial production at the increasing levels of labor productivity. However, rapidly expanding information-related activities created employment at a totally unanticipated rate. As a result, by the 1980s the majority of the workforce in many countries was already employed in information-related work. These countries were already entering the condition often termed "information society," and the other industrializing countries seemed headed in the same direction.

Once again we hear the reassurance that, somehow, demand for these information-related services will increase at such a rate that we need not fear the further job-displacement effects of computer technology, artificial intelligence, and robots. Just give us enough economic growth and everything will be all right. And what will create that consumption, and that growth? INFORMATION!! We can all develop an insatiable appetite for information, to be passed around at an exponentially increasing rate. Never mind that boundless consumption of information services to create jobs may not be the choice of thinking people, anymore than was boundless consumption of food or of manufactured goods. Perhaps instead of "information society" it should be called "makework society."

Some of the characteristics of "information society" are indeed alluring. Information is a clean commodity, compared with coal, steel, and chemicals. We can envision a society in which people work at pleasant jobs, often operating from pleasant work stations in their homes. They have both income and leisure in which to spend it. The attractive pictures of this sort that are painted in articles and books typically overlook the puzzling question of why, with the present economy more productive than ever before in history, increasing numbers of families are finding that they have less leisure and can no longer get along on the wages of one income-earner.

The strategic capital of this attractive society is not so much money as knowledge—technical and managerial know-how. This results in a new ease of access to the economic system and a rise in entrepreneurship based on key information—for example, new cleverness in computer programming or new gene-splicing techniques in biotechnology. Some of these new information organizations are wholly different corporate cultures than the factory, characterized by non-hierarchical management forms and an intellectual environment more like that of a university. (Zuboff, 1988)

The descriptions sound almost idyllic. What is left out, however, is the inherent tendency of this "information society" to become a two-tiered society—the knowledge-rich and the knowledge-poor. Nor does this concept of "information society" address a more fundamental problem: The spectacular success of industrialization and technological advance has brought us to a relatively unnoticed crisis in meaning and values which is as serious as the more obvious crises of global environmental deterioration, nuclear weapons confrontation, and the South's population-poverty dilemma.

So the indications are that evolving to an "information society" does not really solve the work dilemma—certainly not automatically. We will have to search for the resolution of that dilemma in a more fundamental transformation.

The real function of employment. And so we arrive at the hypothetical situation Keynes identified. What if a society advances technologically until it is apparent that economic production of all the goods and services the society can imagine needing or desiring (or that the resources and environment can stand) can be accomplished with ease, using only a small fraction of the population? What then?

As we have seen, the answer so far appears to be to continue attempts to create jobs by stimulating economic growth. Even so, there won't be enough jobs, so those left out will have to be taken care of by transfer payments. In effect, the old ethic of "work in order to eat" seems to be changing to "the fortunate may find work; the remainder will be provided the physical necessities as a basic right." If work is thought of as a scarce commodity that has to be rationed, then approaches such as job-sharing and limitations on the work week seem attractive; at least they seem to be ways of retaining some sort of participation in society's chief preoccupation of economic production.

But all of this overlooks how basic the dilemma really is. Contemporary concepts of business and labor, of employment and welfare theory, of liberal and Marxist analyses, are all based in production-focused society. It is this central concept that is obsolete.

What is required is a new mode of thinking, wherein the widespread elimination of human work which machines can be trained to do is taken as a stimulus to rethink the basic assumptions of production/consumption-focused society—including the assumption that income distribution should be tightly linked to jobs in the mainline economy.

In a technologically advanced society where production of sufficient goods and services can be handled with ease, employment exists primarily for self-development, and is only secondarily concerned with the production of goods and services. "Self-development" is meant here to imply all that enriches the self, including not only personal and professional development, but quality relationships and meaningful service to others.

This redefinition of what work is about comprises the revolutionary thought around which a restructuring of work roles must take place.

The Unrecognized Challenge: Redefining Work

All of history supports the observation that the desire to create is a fundamental urge in humankind. *Fundamentally, we work to create, and only incidentally do we work to eat.* That creativity may be in relationships, communication, service, art, or useful products. It comes close to being the central meaning of our lives.

Until recently in the West, the most important question to be asked of a man was: What is your vocation? That is, where do you create? (It was not necessary to ask the question of a woman since it could be assumed that the arena for her creating was the family and the home.) In traditional societies, particularly those of indigenous peoples, the creation was collective, and participation was through ritual and communal work. One of the great disservices of the modern paradigm is that it obscured the fact of our creative urge, and persuaded us that we really are economically motivated and work for economic reward. (Of course we must not overlook the fact that hunger and destitution can obscure the creative urge as well.)

During the earlier part of the industrial period the collective work, the "central project," of Western society was oriented around material progress, just as surely as during the Middle Ages it centered around building great cathedrals for the glory of God. Over the past half century, however, a "central project" of mere economic growth and technological advance, unguided by overarching values, seems decreasingly suitable, and the need is sensed to reorient around a new focus.

The new failure of jobs to perform their time-honored functions. We have argued earlier that modern society needs to rethink the role of work. In approaching this issue it is helpful to remind ourselves of the functions that education and work together have performed historically. Essentially, these are four:

1. Promoting the *learning and development* of the individual citizen;
2. Providing the individual with a *social role* in the meaningful activities of society, with the opportunity to achieve a sense of contributing, belonging, and being appreciated, thereby developing healthy self-esteem;
3. *Producing* needed and desired goods and services for society;
4. *Distributing the total income* of the society in a way that is generally perceived as equitable.

In the past these four functions have been delegated largely to schools (learning and development), parents and peer groups (development and social roles), and jobs (all four).

In recent decades this arrangement has become progressively less effective. The production economy has difficulty providing an adequate number of suitably challenging work roles for the ever-increasing educational levels. Through increasing labor productivity, it is no longer true that all of the potential labor force is needed to produce the goods and conventional services to fill previously felt needs. The "solution" in the recent past was for us to "need" more. But limitless consumption, even of services, eventually runs into difficulties with resource and environmental limits and consumer resistance.

Furthermore, jobs in the mainstream economy have become progressively less satisfactory as an equitable basis for income distribution. As labor productivity is raised through capital-intensive technology, each worker can apparently produce more wealth. However, as the process of industrialization has proceeded, the increases in wealth are less and less the contribution of routine, narrowly trained, or unskilled labor, and increasingly the contribution of capital and highly skilled technical work embedded in the production machines. Nevertheless, the real wages of unskilled or semi-skilled laborers have risen as fast as, or faster than, the wages of managers and technically creative workers. Thus wage levels have become quite divorced from the real value added by the worker. John Naisbitt (as Daniel Bell before him) says it is time for Marx's "labor theory of value" to be replaced by a new "knowledge theory of value." And perhaps it is time to frankly abandon the idea that the individual's compensation should be directly tied to his or her identifiable contribution to the economic output.

In response to the manifest inequities of income distribution according to productivity, and to the persistence of unemployment and "unemployability" of some workers, the government's role in redistributing income has grown vastly in most countries. Governmental redistribution is accomplished by direct transfer payments, such as social security and public assistance programs; by the graduated income tax and other differential monetary and fiscal policies; and by controls on wages, prices, and interest rates. These policies have weakened still further the link between wage levels and the individual's contribution to direct value added.

For all practical purposes, the notion that an individual's income is determined by the productivity of his or her labor (plus return from property) has become obsolete. As a substitute, society has been confusedly attempting to rationalize income distribution with vaguely defined principles of welfare and equity. Work is still the least controversial form of income distribution, but it has been becoming steadily less and less suitable for that purpose.

A similar situation exists with regard to the social function of work. Work is one of the most socially acceptable, potentially constructive ways for people to spend the major portion of their waking hours. But in the consumption-focused industrial economy, deeply satisfying work opportunities tend to be in increasingly scarce supply.

Finally, the old concept of education as job preparation is totally unsatisfactory from both the standpoints of the individual and society. For a host of reasons, lifelong learning is the only kind of education that makes sense. Thus, the workplace can also be considered as a learning place. But the economy has difficulty adjusting to that idea. According to its rules, work is something you get paid to do, and education is something you *pay for*.

Toward a solution to the work dilemma. From the above discussion, the dilemma can now be reframed. The problem is to so redefine the four functions of work and education that the unsatisfactory aspects are eliminated.

We remind ourselves that we are dealing with *a problem of success.* In terms of its own goals of efficiency, labor productivity, material advance, and consumption, industrialization must be judged an unqualified success. From an economic standpoint, the production problem has been solved once and for all.

If human beings basically sought to escape from work, industrialization might be considered a success from a social and humane standpoint as well, since it has made possible the elimination of so much of the chore work that humans once had to do. But both from observation of worker behavior and from the findings of psychological research, there is ample evidence that *persons basically seek meaningful activities and relationships.* Humans thrive not on mindless pleasure, but on challenge. *Thus, although full employment is no longer needed from a production standpoint, full participation is essential from a social standpoint.*

As we have seen, the processes of production will eventually fail to provide enough work roles either for satisfactory fulfillment of the income-distribution function or the social-roles function. There appear to be two fundamentally different ways in which this situation might be approached.

1) The transfer-payments approach. One of these is essentially a top-down transfer-payments approach. The term transfer payment usually refers to income payments and transfers of purchasing power by governments to people deemed needy or worthy (or both). If the economists' usual definition is broadened to include transfers from institutions and individuals as well as governments, well over half the populations of most modern countries are already supported wholly or in large part by transfer payments. (These are mostly housewives, children, and students.)

In this broader definition, there are at least four distinct kinds of transfer payments:

1. Those based on *membership*, entitling a person to support simply by virtue of belonging to a particular group such as the family, community, organization, or society (for example, child support);

2. Those that are a *social investment* on promise (such as research fellowships and competitive scholarships);

3. Those based on *need*, but *conditional* (such as substitutes for welfare where in order to receive payment persons must propose and carry out socially constructive tasks);

4. Those based on *need*, but *unconditional* (welfare and unemployment payments, assistance to the aged).

It is rather generally agreed that the fourth kind of transfer payment is often accompanied by deleterious social consequences. People do not thrive through being "kept." Both the third and fourth have mixed effects when, as is often the case, they are carried out in a highly centralized manner, administered by a multi-layered bureaucratic structure. Probably much more could be done with the first three. The first, distribution on the basis of membership, works particularly well when the group is small and bonded by other ties, such as family or religious commitment; in Chapter 6 we will look briefly at the Mondragon cooperatives which exemplify this principle. Much more could constructively be done with the second kind of distribution, on the basis of promise, which appears to be especially beneficial in its effects when supported on a very decentralized basis, by private philanthropy.

One of the most ambitious ways of redistributing on the basis of membership is the guaranteed income sort of proposal, pioneered by British economist Robert Theobald. The basic concept is that everyone is entitled, by virtue of membership in society alone, to a basic income, or sharing of the total national product.

2) Toward a "learning society." The second approach involves a much more fundamental transformation of society. It appears feasible because of the question toward which the above discussion of work leads us, namely: *When it no longer makes sense for an economically* *and technologically successful society to have economic production (and consumption) as its central focus, what then becomes that society's "central project"?* There seems to be only one satisfactory answer: *learning and human development*, in the broadest possible sense—as end as well as means. Learning about self, health, meaning in life; learning skills to be used in service or productive creation; learning that the potentialities for learning are endless. What acceptance of this answer would mean for the restructuring of society is a discussion that we shall defer to Chapter 4.

The Special Role of Business Leadership

It is especially important for business leadership to understand the sorts of issues raised in the above discussion. In modern society, business, with its associated technological capabilities, is a powerful shaping force of the future. Business creates most of the jobs in capitalist societies. Business has attracted a fair proportion of the most creative persons in society. The modern corporation is as adaptable an organizational form as has ever been invented, so that in a time of fundamental change it may be expected to be on the cutting edge.

We have earlier noted the tendency among those employed in modern business and industry to desire a work environment that promotes creative initiative and meaningful participation. As competition for excellent talent intensifies, one of the most significant factors in attracting and holding the very best people will be the quality of work environment.

Not only is a spontaneous awakening taking place, especially among the professional and entrepreneurial groups; it is abetted, in the more forward-looking companies, by a variety of personal development seminars and courses. These courses often are built around two key experiential insights which are more revolutionary than may be immediately apparent. One is the awareness and cultivation of personal empowerment, the proposition that *you can create what you choose.* The second is the discovery of one's own deep wisdom and understanding of the truth of the times; of access to inner resources that both guide the choice and contribute to its accomplishment.

Both of these insights are rooted in a picture of reality very different from the official one taught in school curricula and science courses. This picture involves a much more intimate sense of the whole, in which everything is connected to everything else, and it is obvious that no one really wins unless all do. This perspective also involves a deeper appreciation of the power of inner beliefs, and the possibility of reshaping these through techniques of visualization and affirmation. Because the interconnectedness includes minds at some deep level, the potentiality of intuition and creative imagination is far more unlimited than one would infer from a model in which the mind-brain system is assumed to be some sort of computer confined within the individual cranium. Awareness of the expanded nature of these inner resources leads to a shift in the individual's perceived source of authority, away from external dogmas and "experts" of all kinds, and toward deepened trust in the inner, intuitive authority.

As this sense of self-empowerment and inner authority spreads, the meaning of management and leadership changes. Management becomes much more a matter of encouraging others to develop and use their own creativity; leadership has a great deal to do with bringing forth the guiding vision in the collective.

The near-term future is going to be a time of redefining the world. Since business has become the predominant institution in modern society, it will inevitably have a strong hand in that reshaping. A key element has to do with society's ability to help the individual find his or her "creative work." The involvement with these critical issues is the "creative work" of business.

Chapter 2

The Complex Origins of Modern Dilemmas

The deep-level changes taking place in modern society will involve, fairly centrally, a reassessment of the role of work. Radical changes are occurring because they have to: Modern society is approaching the end of its tether. As a reminder of the truth of this assertion, this chapter reviews some of the major societal and global dilemmas and their multi-leveled causes.

In the last few years we have all become aware of these dilemmas. This is not the place for detailed analysis of, or further agonizing over, the problems. But we need to understand fully the extent of their interconnectedness; of their comprising a single, far more fundamental, whole-system problem. Mikhail Gorbachev discovered after two years of attempted moderate reform that would not be sufficient to solve the problems of the Soviet Union; a much more thoroughgoing *perestroika* would be required. We are in process of learning a similar lesson with regard to the global system.

The Interconnectedness of Global Problems

One commonly hears, these days, the observation that "everything is connected to everything else." Although the truth of the statement is evident, discussion seldom progresses to the point where the implications for action are clear.

The sample of major problems afflicting the world which are explored below illustrate this interconnectedness. We cannot attempt to be comprehensive in that exploration; nevertheless the deeper-level interpretations with which we conclude this chapter would be supported by a more inclusive analysis. They comprise a summary argument for considering the necessity of whole-system change.

Man-made climate change. The reality of human-caused climate change has finally penetrated the awareness threshold. Even the most casual reader of the world press has heard of the "greenhouse effect" and the depletion of the ozone layer.

The climate of the Earth is largely determined by its heat balance. Most of the sun's energy that reaches the Earth is in the form of radiation in the visible light and near-ultraviolet band of the spectrum, to which the atmosphere is nearly transparent. Absorption of this energy warms the Earth's surface, and some of the heat is re-radiated as infrared radiation. But the atmosphere is not nearly so transparent to these longer wavelengths. Various gases in the air—especially carbon dioxide, water vapor and droplets, and methane—absorb this infrared energy and reradiate about half of it back to the Earth's surface. This phenomenon of heating, which is due to the differential transparency of the atmosphere to long and short wavelengths of electromagnetic radiation, is called the "greenhouse effect," since the glass of a greenhouse performs a similar function. If this "trapping" of heat did not occur, the surface of the Earth would have an average temperature of around -23° C instead of its present +15° C.

In recent years this "greenhouse effect" has intensified significantly because of a number of factors associated with industrial society. Waste disposal in the air and in the oceans, the burning of fossil fuels to supply energy, gaseous by-products of industrial and agricultural production, the widespread destruction of the Earth's forest cover, all contribute to the change in the balance of atmospheric gases. This change in the chemical balance of the atmosphere, especially the rapid increase of carbon dioxide, is at the heart of the global warming trend which some scientists predict may result in an increase in average temperature of five to eight degrees by the middle of the next century.

The large-scale combustion of fossil fuels is a major factor in adding carbon dioxide and other gases to the atmosphere. So also is the burning of solid waste. The landfills which once took care of the leftover stuff of modern society are either full or unsuited to hold toxic materials which leach out and contaminate groundwater. But when this material is burned instead of buried, this too contributes to the atmospheric imbalance.

At the same time, all this combustion adds particulate matter to the atmosphere, increasing the albedo (the fraction of incoming light that is directly reflected) and bringing about a cooling influence.

(This tendency, as a number of researchers have noted, would be greatly exaggerated in the event of a nuclear war, and has been written about as "nuclear winter.") Furthermore, the added moisture from tropical warming tends to migrate to the polar regions and bring about cloudcover, cooling, and precipitation; already there are indications that the ice sheets of Antarctica and Greenland are deepening at the rate of several feet per year.

The fact that there are simultaneous heating and cooling effects of the greenhouse effect adds to the uncertainty about what the net consequence may be. In fact, we aren't sure whether we are going to be roasted and parched, or suffer another Ice Age.

The prodigious waste production of industrial society contributes yet another influence on the climate. Spewing out of the world's industrial processes and waste incinerators come something like 20 billion tons a year of dissolved and suspended matter that reaches the oceans through river discharge, runoff, waste dumping, offshore mining and shipping accidents. This directly assaults the oceans' phytoplankton population which is critical to regulation of the atmospheric composition through carbon dioxide absorption.

Also under assault are the world's forests, which both transmute atmospheric carbon dioxide into oxygen and affect climate through transpiration. The tropical rainforests are especially important because of their massive capability to supply oxygen to the atmosphere and drain off carbon dioxide; because of this they are sometimes called "the lungs of the Earth." Over half of the tropical rainforests that existed a few centuries ago are already lost to human activities; another quarter of what remains may disappear before the end of the century. Because the favored means of clearing the forests is slash and burn, there is an additional impact of vast quantities of particulate matter being added to the atmosphere.

The bottom line of all this is that the activities of industrial and industrializing societies are having unpredictable effects on the world's climate patterns, and these seem destined to increase. Because it takes time for plant life to adapt to changed conditions, any *rapid* change in climate patterns is bound to reduce food production. Thus, as a result of the greenhouse effect, agricultural productivity of many areas could shift dramatically, with the likelihood of regional food shortages and resulting international tensions and instability. Furthermore, this effect is due largely to the *accumulation* of carbon dioxide; any measures to cut back on the rate of generation, or the absorption, of carbon dioxide would take many years to have much affect on the accumulated total.

A few moments' thought about the horrendous economic impact of cutting back sharply on fossil fuel use, considering the myriad of ways in which our economy is dependent on coal, oil, and natural gas, yields the conclusion that this is not likely to happen. This is not to preclude the possibility, of course, of "buying time" through legislation to increase efficiency of energy use, to promote use of alternative energy sources, or through other measures slow down the inexorable greenhouse effect. Even attempts to slow down the destruction of tropical rainforests, or to accomplish global reforestation, encounter severe economic and political difficulties.

Thus, although the ultimate costs of not acting quickly to meet these climate modification challenges may be very great, the economic and political obstacles to doing so are also huge.

Economic growth. The economic growth problem is usually posed: How can we get more of it? But the more penetrating question is: How can we learn to get along without it? (Daly, 1977)

The U.S. economy has on the whole been quite strong since World War II. This would have surprised many observers in the year 1945, when an often-heard and ominous question was what would happen "when peace breaks out." The threat of dropping back into a second-phase Great Depression seemed very real. Of course that didn't happen. The reason it didn't was because several changes took place.

One of these changes was that over the next couple of decades the U.S. became a debtor society. People who previously had an ethic of saving until they could afford to buy now learned to "buy now, pay later." Corporations shifted from financing through issuing stock to financing through loans; debt replaced equity. Municipal and national governments found deficit financing politically more attractive than taxing adequately as they went along.

Another, related shift had to do with the acceptance of high interest rates. At an earlier time there had been two words in use with quite different connotations. "Interest" was a reasonable fee charged for a loan, whereas "usury" meant profiteering from moneylending. The distinction disappeared, and charging interest at what would once have been considered usurious rates became commonplace.

The *combined effect* of a debtor psychology and high interest rates has a particularly pernicious consequence in the long run. The immediate effect has been that for every dollar a household spends,

30 to 50 cents go to debt servicing, most of it hidden. Everybody, rich and poor alike, gives out a third to half of total expenditures in direct and indirect interest payments. However, a small minority have excess money to lend out so that they *receive* interest. The net effect is of a pervasive and pernicious redistribution system, steadily shifting money from the working and middle classes to the rich. Over time, this unfair tendency of the economy to concentrate wealth is bound to result in mass discontent and political instability. A similar mechanism operates between nations, where its effect is already apparent in the fact that for many developing countries the transfer of wealth from poor nation to rich in the form of debt servicing far exceeds the transfer in the reverse direction through trade and development aid.

With the beginning of the Cold War, the military sector became a new factor in the economies of the "advanced" nations of Europe and North America. National security became dominated by the concept that more weapons equals more security. The economy became inextricably linked with military policy and arms production; so much so that in the U.S., well over half the federal budget currently goes to military spending, and two fifths of all engineers and three quarters of all scientists are working in defense related jobs. Employment levels and military spending are not separable issues.

The United States and the Soviet Union are the leading exporters of armaments. This reveals another, even deeper shift in the realm of ethics. As recently as the late 1930s, the sale of weapons to other countries by the U.S. would have been considered morally outrageous. Some readers will recall that when the United States wanted to assist beleaguered Britain prior to World War II by giving them some old U.S. destroyers, it had to be done under the gloss of "Lend-Lease." One of the most serious charges made against the Germany of the early twentieth century was that it condoned profiteering from the sale of arms to other nations. Yet in the U.S. by the mid-1950s the exporting of arms was quite an accepted practice and before long became a significant fraction of the total exports of the U.S. economy. Europe, especially France and Sweden, as well as the Soviet Union, are major arms suppliers. Thus the global arms race is intrinsically linked to employment issues in the U.S. and Europe alike.

But perhaps the most important of the post-war changes amounted to a significant change in cultural values. Frugality had been a virtue; consuming more than necessary was mildly sinful.

After around 1950 consumption became the virtue and frugality was deemed bad for the economy. The United States became, proudly, a "Throwaway Society." People learned how to waste; how to use and discard disposables from drapes to dishes; how to become dissatisfied with last year's automobile or appliance and demand the new model. They learned about "planned obsolescence." Persons were referred to, no longer as "citizens," but as "consumers." The resulting consumption boom more than compensated for the dropping off of war contracts and more than took care of the job-seekers returning from the war.

Markets for some products were saturated: There is a limit, for example, to how many refrigerators or vacuum cleaners a family needs. Furthermore, increasing automation of industrial production reduced the labor content of goods. The combination of these two factors brought a basic change in the nature of the U.S. economy. By the mid-1950s the number of white-collar and service workers exceeded the number of blue-collar workers for the first time, and the fraction of the workforce engaged in manufacturing began to decline. Concurrently, the percentage of workers engaged in the service sector increased; this was particularly true for those involved with information services.

This related to another cultural shift, away from being a society in which gambling was frowned upon and rather generally forbidden, to one in which it is a way of life. State after state discovered that running a lottery is a painless way to raise money without generating taxpayer resistance. Wall Street became more a place of speculation than of investment, with large pension funds and insurance companies among the major players. The "financial industry" employs a lot of people in financial services but contributes little in terms of real wealth. No one exactly calls it a "makework" sector, but...

All of these factors contributed to the strength of the U.S. and European economies in the post-war years, but they had serious long-range implications. The combination of increasing labor productivity, loss of some markets to overseas competition, the entry of new participants, especially women, into the workforce, and the psychology of investors and workers expecting ever-increasing return, all put pressure on the economy to grow and to create new jobs. The rate of increase of GNP became the accepted measure of the health of the economy. But that measure is highly correlated with the rate at which the economy consumes scarce resources, and the rate at which it creates environmental degradation. In other words, inadvertently *the economic incentives structure came to favor resource depletion and spoliation of the environment.*

The pressure to create jobs no matter what consequences ensue leads society to promote superfluous production and consumption; to see economic benefits in high "national security" expenditures; and to view approvingly an ever-growing "financial industries" sector which generates jobs but contributes nothing in terms of basic goods or services. In addition, there is a tendency to accept the environmental and resource depletion consequences of these policies as unavoidable, as symptoms which can perhaps be dealt with through ameliorative measures.

The emphasis on economic growth and its most widely used measure, the GNP, leads to a warping of social priorities. Financial speculation, non-reusable containers, extravagant packaging and advertising, wasteful energy use, the "gambling industry" of Las Vegas and Atlantic City, all presumably add to the GNP and strengthen the economy. On the other hand, providing good education for all, beautification of the environment, or assuring citizen protection in urban environments are included in public-sector expenditures and supposedly represent drains on the economy.

In sum, the sociopolitical demand for jobs drives the economy in some ways that are ultimately detrimental to the planet, to the social integrity, and to the well-being of future generations. While the above discussion focused on the U.S. and Western Europe, similar observations could be made about all the industrialized world. Practically all the industrialized countries are by now mass consumption societies; practically all have the same pressure to create economic growth and jobs. The extent to which speculation has become a major factor in the world economy is indicated by two figures: World trade annually comes to about $3 trillion; world financial flows per year are around $80 trillion! It is finance, not agricultural and industrial production, that drives the world economy. The world has become one vast gambling casino, and most of the money exchange has nothing whatever to do with constructive goods and services.

Agriculture and food production and distribution. A particular part of the economy—agriculture, and the production and distribution of food and other agricultural products—merits special attention because it is here that the modern economy is most out of consonance with the natural order. It is not just that agribusiness went overboard with its use of pesticides and artificial fertilizers, and has made it hard for the family farm to survive; the long-term trouble lies deeper.

Wendell Berry (1978) has been one of the foremost critics of our present approach to agriculture. He argues, first of all, that agriculture cannot be understood and dealt with as an industry. The economy of industry is extractive; it takes, makes, uses, and discards; it progresses from exhaustion to pollution. Agriculture, on the other hand, rightly belongs to a replenishing economy, which takes, makes, uses, and returns. It involves the return to the source, not just of fertility, of so-called "wastes," but of care and affection. Otherwise, the soil is used exactly as a mineable fuel, and is destroyed in use. The old farming ethic involved passing the land on to future generations in an improved, not a depleted state.

The farmer, unlike the industrialist, is necessarily a nurturer, a preserver of the health of creatures. Topsoil, unlike factories, need not wear out; some has been in continuous use for thousands of years. The motives of the wage earner are inadequate to farming; love of land and animals is an essential factor.

Furthermore, Berry argues, a sound agricultural economy cannot be based on an export market. The farm family should, as far as possible, live off the land, which can provide food, shelter, fuel, and building materials. The local consumer population should subsist, so far as possible, from the produce of the locality or region. The same should be true at the national level. Only then can agriculture be carried out on the basis of local, that is, mainly solar energy, sources. With the present system of mass production of agricultural products and transportation to distant markets, when the energy costs of tractor fuels, fertilizers, transportation, processing, packaging, freezing, thawing, and the like are counted in, the food on your table represents something like eight to twelve times as much fossil fuel energy as solar energy. Such a situation is clearly not viable in the long term.

Another problem has to do with economic incentives. American agriculture is fantastically productive in terms of output per person-hour or output per acre of land. However, it is also fantastically expensive in terms of loss of soil, in loss of farms and alienation of farmers, in soil and water pollution, in food pollution, in the decay of country towns and communities, and in the increasing vulnerability of the food supply system. The "free market" is unable to assign a value to many factors vital to sound agriculture, such as topsoil, ecosystem, family, community. The excessive emphasis on production not only creates the effects just mentioned; it also inevitably causes over-production—which leads to low prices and economic ruin.

Governments try to deal with this latter problem with such devices as subsidies, paying farmers to let land lay idle, and buying up surplus crops. But the problem lies deeper than that. From an ecological and humane standpoint, the guiding ethic in agriculture needs to be thrift—to be *thrifty* insofar as one's land, crops, animals, place, and community are thriving. But when agriculture is treated as an industry like other industries, the economic incentives foster the wrong sorts of behavior. Furthermore, those who farm with concern for the health of the land and the long-term future tend to be put out of business by those who concentrate on production over the short term.

One element of the situation is the psychological impact of labor-saving technology. Once one has experienced the tractor with air-conditioned cab, one is unlikely to be content following a horse with a plow. The work no longer has the same meaning. However, there is a profound truth in Berry's observation that hand labor is not something to be avoided because it is wearisome or beneath one's dignity. The pleasantness or unpleasantness of hand labor depends on such factors as the cultural value put on relationship to nature, the context of meaning created by the farming community, the size of the crop, having good tools, and ownership.

Chronic poverty and maldevelopment. One of the greatest potential forces for fundamental change in the global system is the "sleeping giant" known as the developing world. The giant is awakening: Those who had, for so long, accepted the role of privation, inferiority, and servility are less and less willing to do so. From accepting widespread poverty and hunger as conditions which fate has dealt, they increasingly see them as unacceptable features of a global system which can and must be changed.

For the two decades following World War II, democratic liberation and economic development were the two chief political themes. Development was more or less taken to be synonymous with economic development, that is, with "modernization" and industrialization.

One of the main efforts of this development thrust was to alleviate hunger. The "Green Revolution," the development of high-yield grains that were to spell the end of hunger for hundreds of millions, proved a mixed success. Yields did increase and more people were fed; but population continued to grow, and land ownership and political power remained concentrated in a very few hands. The net effect in many regions was that the opportunity for a family to grow its own food and sell produce from its own land actually diminished. The effect has been exacerbated where "cash crops" for export have displaced produce grown for local consumption.

Increasingly, political and cultural leaders in developing countries have come to see that the best development for them is not necessarily abandonment of their own cultural roots and adoption of the alien culture of Western industrial society. There has been growing insistence not only on a different international economic order, but also on exploring alternative development paths.

One key dimension of the global development issue is that of needs satisfaction and equity. In a series of documents from the International Labour Organization and other United Nations agencies relating to demands for a "New International Economic Order," a set of universally felt human needs has been defined:

- Basic human needs ("enough" food, shelter, health care, education, employment, and security of the person).
- A sense of the dignity of being human.
- A sense of becoming (a chance to achieve a better life).
- A sense of justice or equity.
- A sense of achievement, of being able to accomplish something worth achieving.
- A sense of solidarity, of belonging to a worthy group and of participation in decisions that affect the group's, and one's own, destiny.

National-level programs aimed at guaranteeing the right to satisfaction of these universal needs have been adopted by over 120 countries, in most cases within the past forty years. In some of the countries, including the United States, the programs were preceded by years of debate over the appropriateness of such guarantees and the kinds of programs and payments involved. Behind the rhetoric of the demands for a new economic order is the proposition that the concept of welfare that has thus far been accepted and applied within a majority of individual nations *should now be extended to the entire family of humankind*. Despite inevitable opposition, ultimate acceptance of this proposition appears likely, in that it is an extension of an already accepted basic trend.

This amounts to much more than a mere adjustment of the existing economic institutions for more equitable distribution. It implies no less than a restructuring of international society around a newly recognized fundamental right, as profound in its ultimate implications as was the concept of democratic government two centuries ago.

A crucial factor limiting the extension of human rights will be population pressure. World population is presently approximately 5 billion people; projections put it at around 8.5 billion by the year 2035. More people means more pollution, more habitat destruction, and more social unrest; this is probably the case even assuming the maximum likely changes in basic economic expectations and structures, and maximum likely adoption of population reduction measures.

Whether or not the pressure for a "new economic order" grows or declines, the basic situation remains. It is by no means obvious that the global system in anything like its present form is viable in the long term, or that it leads toward either an ecologically sustainable society or a satisfactory resolution to the plight of the poorest countries. Nor is it clear how basic a change would be required for it to do so.

The global dilemma can be simply stated. *Of the easily imaginable paths of global development, those that appear to be economically feasible do not look to be ecologically and socially plausible, and those that appear ecologically feasible and humanely desirable do not seem economically and politically feasible.*

To illustrate, imagine that all the developing countries were to be successful in following the examples of the industrialized and newly industrializing countries, assumed in the 1950s and 1960s to be the "normal" course of development. The planet would be hard-pressed to accommodate 6 to 8 billion people living high-consumption lifestyles, and it is easy to imagine intense political battles over environmental and quality-of-life issues. We may try to picture another path where the presently high-consumption societies remain so, but the poorer countries stay low-consumption, that is, poor, with low per capita demand on resources and environment. It is hard to see how a global system with such a persisting disparity of income and wealth could avoid vicious "wars of redistribution," with terrorism and sabotage among the main weapons. A third conceivable path in which high-consumption societies voluntarily cut consumption to ameliorate some of the problems is equally difficult to imagine, partly because of the severe unemployment problems those societies would face. A path to global socialist hegemony has had some popularity among developing nations in the past, but it is totally unacceptable to the capitalist nations and is losing favor even in those countries where it was once strong.

No consensus exists today regarding what constitutes a viable pattern of global development. It is increasingly clear that present trends do *not* lead to a viable future. The present global system, and the assumptions which underlie it, appear in the end to be incompatible with a wise relationship to the Earth and its resources; to systematically produce marginal people who have no meaningful roles in the society; to create societies that habitually confuse goals with means (economic and technological achievement); and to persistently endanger the future with a militarization which is an intrinsic part of the system and diverts resources from the real satisfaction of human needs. The present global system offers little hope to those in the developing countries caught in the fourfold web of deprivation: poverty; debt; cash crops for export in the midst of hunger; and local environmental deterioration (overgrazing, forest destruction for firewood, soil erosion and removal of humus [dung] for fuel, surface water contamination).

The central theme throughout the discussion of this entire section can be summarized in one telling observation: *Present economic, corporate, and social policies are, by and large, inconsistent with viable long-term global development, and are being everywhere made without a picture of a viable global future in mind, or an understanding of the global system change required to bring about such a future.* This is the predicament of the contemporary world.

Contributing Factors from the Past

To really understand this predicament, it is necessary to inquire into its origins. When seeking an explanation as to why the world is in its present state, it makes a great difference what time interval is used for viewing. If one thinks of trends that have been evident in Western Europe and North America since around the end of World War II (about half a century), certain things stand out. If instead the focus is on the period since the Middle Ages (roughly, three and a half centuries), other factors emerge as critically important. (These are discussed immediately below.) Again, if one looks with a time span of millennia rather than centuries, then the factors that stand out are things like the agricultural revolution, the rise of cities, and, particularly, the emergence of patriarchal society with values and assumptions that have dominated Western society for the past five thousand years, until challenged by the recent emergence of the women's movement. All of these factors contribute to the ultimate explanation of how we got to our present situation, and of the whole-system change required to reach satisfactory resolution of our manifold problems and dilemmas.

Thus, while some of the factors that contribute to the present state of the world arise out of changes that have taken place over the last half century, the problem cannot be seen adequately without bringing in at least two longer-term factors: (a) the full import of the "modernization" trend that set in with the ending of the Middle Ages in Western Europe; and (b) the influence of patriarchal society.

The "modernization" revolution of the seventeenth century. The seventeenth-century developments in Western Europe not only marked the ending of the Middle Ages there, they ultimately had an impact on practically every area of the globe.

It is not too great a simplification to say that the fundamental thing that happened in this century was that the prevailing "picture of reality" changed from a medieval one to one we would recognize as at least proto-modern. In medieval reality the Earth was the center of the cosmos—the seat of change, decay, and Christian redemption. Above it circled the luminous heavenly bodies, themselves pure and unchanging, but moved by divine spirits and signaling and influencing human events by their locations and aspects. The universe was alive and imbued with purpose. All creatures were seen to be part of a Great Chain of Being, with man between the angels and the lower animals. Events were explained by divine purpose or by their function in a meaningful world.

An educated man in 1600 would still have perceived the medieval cosmos; by 1700 his counterpart would literally have perceived a different reality. Where the universe of stars and planets had been alive, it was now essentially dead: initially constructed and set in motion by the Creator, with subsequent events accounted for by mechanical forces and lawful behaviors. The Earth was known to be but one of many planets circling around one of many stars, moving through and separated by unimaginable distances. The natural resources and the diverse creatures of the Earth were put here for man's use. On the one hand, man and the planet Earth were removed from their special position at the center of creation; on the other hand, man's destiny was beginning to be seen as unlimited material and moral advance. The concept of material progress, in particular, was coming increasingly strongly into focus.

The seventeenth century was the time of Galileo and Newton; we usually think of it as the era of the scientific revolution. But other important things were going on as well. This period encompassed the latter part of the Reformation and the rise of Puritanism in England. It saw the first of the liberal-democratic revolutions that were to remake most of the governments of the world. And it saw the rise of capitalist philosophy and institutions. It was a time of tremendous controversies in religion, philosophy, and social theory, which set the tenor of the modern mind. It was a great historical watershed. Prior to this were half a dozen centuries of the period we call broadly the Middle Ages. After the impact of the Copernican revolution in the early decades of the seventeenth century, the course was irrevocably set for what we now call the modern era.

Among the persistent themes of the modern, Western industrial-era paradigm are:

- The *scientific method* as the supreme mode of inquiry. The search for scientific knowledge has come to be predominantly utilitarian: Its guiding values are prediction and control and ability to manipulate the physical environment. Although it was not so initially, the ultimate goal of most present-day science is technological advance.
- *Unlimited material progress* as the inherent goal. The paradigm implies belief in man's expanding control over nature; and in his unlimited ability to understand the universe from the data provided by the physical senses. Acquisitive materialism is a central operative value.
- *Industrialization* of the production of goods and services, achieved by subdividing work into increasingly elemental (and less intrinsically meaningful) increments, and replacing human labor by machines. The goals of industrialization are increasing labor productivity and wealth, presumably leading to a higher material standard of living for all.
- *Pragmatic values* predominate, with individuals free to seek their own self-interest in the marketplace. Hence the future is not defined by tradition nor achieved through organized plan,

but rather it happens as a consequence of relatively autonomous units in the system pursuing their own practical ends.

One of the features of this paradigm is the increasing monetization of society. More and more of human activities take place within the mainstream economy, and are valued in economic terms. Increasingly a person defines himself or herself by relationship to the economy, either by job, spouse's job, or job-in-training. Gradually, the economic and financial institutions came to be the paramount institutions. Economic production became (except in time of war) the central concern of society, and economic growth the primary measure by which societies judge their progress.

In *The Transformations of Man* (1956) Lewis Mumford vividly summarizes the vast change that was involved in shifting from the old feudal paradigm of the Middle Ages to the new, industrial-era paradigm: "Within the span of a few centuries the focus of interest shifted from the inner world to the outer world.... All but one of the [seven deadly] sins, sloth, was transformed into a virtue. Greed, avarice, envy, gluttony, luxury, and pride were the driving forces of the new economy.... Unbounded power was harnessed to equally unbounded appetites."

By the latter part of the twentieth century the technological power of the industrialized societies was awesome, and its benefits were impressive. Equally impressive is a fundamental observation whose implications we are only now beginning to grasp: *Most of today's critical societal and global problems have come about, directly or indirectly, because of the **successes** of the Western industrial paradigm.*

Characteristics of patriarchal society. Patriarchal society seems to have appeared in the West around 3500 B.C.E., and has been coterminous with the Western civilizational process for the past five thousand years. Its importance as a shaping factor in the Western perception of reality and value is only recently being appreciated.

The agricultural societies which preceded the patriarchal period in the West appear to have been matricentric (mother-centered); some may even have been matrilineal. It appears, from archeological evidence and historical record, that these societies were more egalitarian, democratic, and peaceful than those which succeeded them. This state of affairs gradually gave way to a male-dominated political state in which occupational specialization, commerce, stratification, and militarism developed—apparently due to invading Aryan Indo-European peoples around 3500 B.C.E. (Eisler, 1987) The heritage of the earlier matricentric phase has continued as an undercurrent within Western cultural traditions. Matricentric ways of thinking and their associated rituals carry on an earlier feminine wisdom associated with alchemy, astrology, pagan nature rituals, and the hermetic spiritual teachings. These hidden traditions, once considered by the religious-humanist traditions of Western society to be antiquated and misleading, now need to be reconsidered for the contributions they make to our understanding of the universe, its deeper modes of functioning, and the proper role of the human. They are related to some of the most creative aspects of our civilization. It is through these traditions that we have recovered our understanding of the archetypal world of the unconscious. In their symbolic expression, especially, they enable us to go beyond the rational processes so honored in patriarchal society.

Thomas Berry (1988) identifies the four patriarchal establishments that have dominated Western history over the centuries as the classical empires, the ecclesiastical establishment, the nation-state, and the modern corporation. "However benign our view of these establishments or however brilliant in some of their achievements, we must observe that they have become progressively virulent in their destructive powers, until presently they are bringing about the closing down of all the basic life systems of the planet." As Berry points out, "these four are exclusively male dominated and primarily for fulfillment in terms of the human as envisaged by men. Women had minimal if any consistent role in the direction of these establishments."

The empires, in general, ruled their subjects in an oppressive manner, including in many cases the institution of slavery. Human rights were minimal and consideration of the natural environment non-existent. With their stupendous irrigation and construction feats and their voracious appetites for timber, they often denuded the land and poisoned the soil through salinization.

The Western ecclesiastical establishment was the second patriarchal institution. The church was the single comprehensive, transnational authority in the Western world for more than a thousand years. The main determinant of reality and value in Western civilization was expressed in the belief structures interpreted and presented by the church. The church was the deepest source and support for the patriarchal tradition. The rulership of men in the church (supposedly by divine determination) assured the relegation of women to subordinate status, the denial of integral participation in religious ritual, and the identification of women with wild nature and moral evil. (This is essentially true, despite the ambivalence suggested by the symbol of the Madonna, an idealized personification of the feminine.)

The third patriarchal institution is the nation-state. After the fifteenth century, a transition was made from the feudal states of the medieval period to the monarchies and city republics of the Renaissance and the later period. The legitimacy of the autonomous nation-state, free to do anything on the planet it had the power to do, was more or less ratified by the Treaty of Westphalia at the end of the Thirty Years War. The concept of the nation-state as the primary civilizing force on the planet led to the colonial enterprise, the control of the peoples and lands and resources of the entire globe by the nation-states of the European world. The nation-state became the model for the aggressive use of power in pursuit of the male values of conquest and dominion.

Fourthly, we have the modern corporation—or more precisely, the interconnected private sector comprised of industrial, commercial, and financial corporations, which is so clearly the predominant sector in modern society. Regions without industrial or commercial establishments are seen as backward places, lacking both amenities in the present, and possibilities for the future. Berry's description of the role of the corporation (1988, p. 156) exemplifies the "bad guy" role the corporation has come to represent:

> The corporation is considered the primary instrument of 'progress,' although just what progress means is never clear. The supposition seems to be that the greater the devastation of the natural world through construction of highways, airports, development projects, shopping malls, supermarkets, and corporate headquarters, the closer we are to fulfilling the American Dream. It is precisely through this dream version of a new humanly created wonderworld that the advertising industry brings about that level of heightened consumption upon which the corporation depends for its ever-increasing control over our society and its ever-increasing profits. Through advertising the corporation has gained control over the public media. Through the public media the corporation controls the deepest psychic as well as the most powerful physical forces of the planet.

But it is neither the corporation nor the nation-state that is at the root of our problems; they, like the problems, are consequences of that root, which is a pattern and belief-system that, to some extent, we all buy into.

It is obviously necessary that we move on from patriarchal society to a more gender-balanced form, but we will need to do it together, and it will not serve us well to try to place blame on some villains from whom we could not, in any event, separate ourselves.

Seeing the Need for System Change

There is a natural temptation to seek explanations of society's problems that lead to specific corrective actions; thus there may be little patience with an attempt to understand their deeper-level system origins. To see how the deeper understanding can also lead to actions, of a different sort, let us first consider an analogy from the health field.

A health analogy. Imagine a person who is plagued with a succession of illnesses, which might range from influenza to cardiovascular disease. Some are caused, perhaps, by bacteria or viruses; others are degenerative. They produce an array of symptoms extending from fever and sore throat to chest pains and shortness of breath. A diagnostician undertakes to explain the "causes" of the observable symptoms.

A great step ahead is taken when a collection of symptoms is identified as a particular disease syndrome. From past familiarity with this disease, the physician may be able to "explain" the symptoms, identify the causative agents, and prescribe a cure. This can be done for each identifiable disease.

But there is another level at which this situation can be viewed. The history of a succession of illnesses may be due to an impairment of the body's immune system. That remarkable complex system, which in good health protects the body against all manner of ailments, may not be functioning effectively, so that bacteria or viruses that would ordinarily be warded off manage to invade the body and, further, to weaken it such that it breaks down in other ways as well.

There is a yet deeper level of explanation. The reason the immune system is not functioning properly may be that the person's attitudes toward job, spouse, finances, etc., are leading to a condition of *stress*. The stress contributes to the impairment of the immune system, and all the further consequences of various forms of illness.

The level one is looking at makes a difference with regard to prescription. One may ameliorate the symptoms one by one—something soothing for the throat, aspirin for the fever, and so on. At the disease level, one thinks perhaps in terms of antibiotics. To deal directly with the immune system, a different medication regime may be prescribed. To eliminate the stress, one may have to change one's basic (perhaps unconsciously held) beliefs and lifestyle. (Of course, at the same time one is working with the stress it may still be appropriate to ameliorate the symptoms; one response does not invalidate the other.)

Patients typically manifest a great deal of resistance to recognizing the deeper-level explanation of their health problems, because of its implications of necessary fundamental change. Similarly, people resist seeing the deeper-level explanations for societal problems. If I perceive the problem of the homeless, or environmental degradation, or world hunger, as a problem "out there," it may impel action, but it does not demand that I change in any fundamental way. If on the other hand I perceive the deeper origins of such problems as a belief system which I and others have been subscribing to, I may be forced to re-examine some very fundamental beliefs. That is a less comfortable position.

Levels of Explanation and Prescription

	Example A: Health	Example B: Business/Politics
Level 1	Symptoms	Problems/symptoms
Level 2	Disease syndrome	Complex of interconnected problems
Level 3	Failure of immune system	Self-healing tendencies
Level 4	Stress	Societal stress
Level 5	Fear, insecurity, anxiety	Fear, insecurity, anxiety
Level 6	Basic belief system that engenders fear and anxiety	Collective basic belief system that engenders fear and anxiety

Re-perceiving societal and global problems. As an example, consider the problems of hunger and poverty in a developing country. Bringing in food and clothing may ameliorate a symptom but it does not solve the problem.

Poverty and hunger in this case may be related to the country's decisions to promote cash crops to earn foreign exchange for debt servicing; to its domestic policies such as subsidies which exhaust the national treasury; to endemic illness which weakens the populace and limits their productiveness; to self-serving and corruption in high places; to traditional ethnic or religious hatreds which evoke exorbitant military expenditures; and so on. In other words, there may be multiple contributing causes, and it may take a coordinated set of diverse policies in order to address these.

Or one may conclude that the poverty is chronic and that generating regional poverty is a built-in characteristic of the global system. That conclusion may be very difficult to communicate to others, because by its nature it is not an easily demonstrable thesis, and because it will be a very threatening idea to many. Such a conclusion is likely to get one labeled insensitive or some kind of troublemaker. Obviously, the kind of action one would recommend from this diagnosis would be very different from the usual political proposals. It involves whole-system change. Although examples of such change are found in history, we do not know how to bring it about deliberately in a manner that is not socially disruptive and accompanied by a great deal of human misery. Often the force for such change comes about from widespread discontent, and involves a challenge to the legitimacy of the old order; it may include a dimly perceived vision of a better way. The challenge to leadership is to sense the rising force for change and to move with it appropriately. When the people lead forcefully enough, the leaders have little choice but to follow.

Developments in China and Eastern Europe in 1989 provide illustrative examples. In the latter area rising discontent over political and economic conditions, and swelling demands for liberty and democracy, brought about fundamental changes with surprising lack of violence; by and large leaders bowed to what they sensed was inevitable. In a somewhat similar situation, the Chinese leaders failed to meet the challenge of allowing the necessary system change to take place in a nondisruptive way. Just as many failed to discern the forces for fundamental change building in Eastern Europe, so many fail to see the subtler forces for fundamental change building up in North America, Western Europe, Japan and the global system.

The Underlying Pathogenic Assumptions

Having argued for seeking understanding at the system level, let us now try to identify the underlying assumptions which are at the root of the malfunctioning of modern society, and hence will be at the heart of the necessary system change. We observed above that modern society is beset with innumerable specific problems and symptoms of malfunctioning. At this level social critics deplore, and politicians promise, but nothing much happens. If symptoms are relieved, they reappear in another form, or the problem "solution" brings "unintended consequences" that often turn out to be at least as bad as the original problems.

If we think in more whole-system terms, we can identify intermediate-level problems that are of a more systemic nature. That is to say, they are described as undesirable characteristics of the overall systems, and their solution is imagined in terms of whole-system change. Many times these are not the problems of any one nation or region, but situations where the welfare of the whole of humanity is involved.

Needless to say, there is more than one way to analyze the dilemmas of modern societies, but the following four intermediate-level problems stand out:

Intermediate Problems and Attempted "Solutions"

1. Tendency of world economy to create scarcity of fresh air and water, arable land, and spirit-renewing wilderness; environmental deterioration; ecological crises; toxic substance concentrations; man-made climate change

Nations have not done well at managing their own "commons"— the land, air, water, and space that must be commonly used. The imperative is to move rapidly to some management of the "global commons." "Global commons" means primarily the four environments which are so recognized by international law and custom: the oceans (including the ocean floor); outer space; atmosphere, weather and climate; and the continent of Antarctica. To these must be added the situations where actions within one nation affect the fresh-water rivers and aquifers of another. The most powerful nations have been among the more reluctant to pool sovereignty to accomplish this management.

The usual approach to environmental problems is to try to ameliorate the symptoms directly, and at the same time adjust the legislative and economic incentive structures to foster desirable changes—reduced energy use and substitution of renewable energy sources; reusable containers and other ways to decrease the amount of solid waste created; biodegradability of non-eliminable waste; reduced pollution and impact on ecological systems; decelerated logging of tropical rainforests; etc. Direct legislation may be used to prohibit CFCs, strictly limit toxic waste, and so forth.

One often suggested measure is better economic and social indicators and a more adequate accounting system. The costs and benefits associated with the social and ecological consequences of economic activity are not commensurate with each other, or with money. Nevertheless, there are numerous ways in which a better job could be done of incorporating the costs of "externalities" such as acid rain, soil erosion, solid waste production and deforestation into a systematic framework that could lead to more enlightened decision making. The environmental impact statements (EIS) now required of various projects, to make publicly available information with regard to anticipated impacts of a decision, make no attempt to express these impacts in some common currency; they simply display them to encourage more awareness about overall consequences of deciding to go ahead. Even so, the EIS proves to be a significant achievement toward facilitating citizen participation in the political process.

However, the intrinsic characteristics of the world economy are such that *all of the above tends to be a desperate catch-up attempt*. The problems continue to worsen at a greater rate than the ameliorative measures patch up the effects. Beyond all of these measures, reassessment of the fundamental characteristics of the global economy is necessary. Resistance to this re-examination is extremely strong.

2. Tendency of world economy to create marginal people and marginal cultures; chronic poverty, hunger and maldevelopment

Here the major attempts of the past have been to ameliorate crises as humane considerations dictate. Recently there have been increasing attempts to help individuals and communities help themselves feel more empowered, become more self-sufficient, regenerate group pride, and embark on a development path appropriate to their unique cultural roots.

Nonetheless, there is a natural tendency in any social system for power to accumulate. Those who have political or economic power are in a good position to gain still more power; those with less power tend to be in a progressively poorer position. Within any society there are some institutionalized mechanisms for limiting this tendency. (Obvious examples are recognized civil rights, the graduated income tax, free legal services for the poor.) But there are at the international level only very primitive and ineffective mechanisms. Thus, for example, the degrees of wealth and income disparities that exist between nations are far greater than would be tolerated even within countries having the most notoriously authoritarian and unjust regimes.

It appears to be difficult for the materially rich countries to move beyond the idea that their affluence is a function of their own merit, and to recognize that the conflict-producing tensions in the world will require what Harlan Cleveland has called a "fairness revolution." Some way must be found, in other words, to limit the natural tendency for power to accumulate at the global level, and to empower the poorest of the poor to assure themselves of those human rights without which existence can hardly be termed human living.

3. Crisis of control

Perhaps the ultimate challenge facing humankind today can be summed up in a single question: *We humans have developed consummate technological capability to do almost anything we can imagine wanting to do; can we now develop corresponding ability to choose wisely which things should be done?*

How can we avoid choosing short-term objectives that induce clearly undesirable long-term consequences, such as resumed nuclear arms race, or gross environmental destruction? How can we exercise needed societal control over technology without sacrificing individual liberty?

Industrial society now has the power:

- To change the characteristics of our physical environment, including climate, as well as the plant and animal population of the biosphere.
- To modify the physical characteristics of individual human bodies and the evolutionary development of the human race, by means of biological and genetic engineering.
- To drastically alter social and psychological environments, including people's mental and emotional characteristics.
- To annihilate large segments of the human race and devastate large areas of the Earth.
- To change significantly, in many other ways, the kind of world that is passed on to future generations.

These powers are so awesome that they clearly must be directed and channeled. And yet it is not clear how this control can be exerted without impinging on fundamental characteristics of our free enterprise system and our democratic society. Nor is it clear how to counteract the built-in bias toward favoring short-term benefits so that more consideration is given to long-term consequences of technological choices.

4. Crisis of meaning and values

It has been said in many ways by many people; surveys show it, and people know it: Modern industrial society knows how to do almost anything that can be imagined, and is totally confused about what is worth doing. In contrast to U.S. or European society of a couple of generations ago, the collective today is deeply perplexed and uncertain about meanings and goals. What is modern society about? Technological advance? Material standard of living as measured by the GNP? Keeping what we have regardless of the welfare of those living in other parts of the planet? Contemporary problems with drugs, gambling, inner-city crime, and the homeless are directly related to this confusion.

The intermediate-level solution that seems to be universally proposed for this crisis is education. Why can't we educate people to find meaning in their lives, and a sound basis for personal and social values? Certainly much can be done, in terms of increasing people's self-awareness and sense of their own power, by ways which are exemplified in numerous weekend workshop and seminar situations. The matter is made more difficult by the fact that the prevailing scientific picture of reality tends to be antithetical to personal discoveries that imply ultimate meanings or eternal values.

But it is not enough for people to find individual meaning when they are surrounded by (and despite) a system which does not reflect that meaning. The prevailing meanings and values of that system must also change. A significant fraction of the world has advanced technologically to the point discussed above, where economic production of all the goods and services that society can imagine needing or desiring (or that the resources and environment can stand) can be provided using only a small fraction of the population. It no longer makes sense for the "central project" of society to be economic production and consumption. What, then, is the new "central project" of advanced societies, and what does this imply for global society as a whole?

We repeat again our main theme in delineating these intermediate-level problems: As basic as they may seem, the change necessary to make them resolvable lies at a still deeper level. If the above four systemic problems can be assumed to summarize the most severe challenges we face, what are the underlying assumptions that will need to change as a part of whole-system change? Perhaps we can identify a few of the most important:

Deeper-level Assumptions

1. Predominance of economic institutions and economic rationality

Modern society is characterized by the predominance of economic institutions and economic rationality. For us who have grown up taking this for granted, it may be difficult to imagine that things might be otherwise. Other long-lived societies in history have had as their paramount institutions those that dealt with knowledge, meaning, humane or spiritual goals; no other society has been so focused around economic production and consumption. No other society has attempted to guide a society with decisions shaped primarily by economic considerations. No other society has taken as its highest value acquisitive materialism.

In the first place, there is no reason whatever to assume that economic rationality will lead to decisions that are wise from human, ecological, compassionate, and spiritual standpoints. As a matter of experience, it doesn't. Whereas the Iroquois tradition was to make decisions having in mind the welfare of those who will live seven generations hence, contemporary decisions—profoundly affecting future generations and people around the globe—are guided by next quarter's financial bottom line, or the way the next electorate will perceive the state of the economy.

Furthermore, the economic and technological values that dominate modern society are really pseudo-values. They only seem like values because of a confusion of means—technology and economic institutions—with ends. And that confusion arises when true ends, which are always transcendental, become obscured through the power given to a materialistic worldview.

2. Nationalism and the concept of "national security"

The rise of the nation-state from the seventeenth century onward brought order out of chaos in many parts of the world. The industrializing nation-state was an extremely effective kind of organization for its own purposes, and few could look ahead to realize that there was an intrinsic contradiction in the long term. The advance of technology inevitably made the world smaller and the problems more global. At the same time, it was clear that certain types of problems involving the well-being of individuals and families could best be handled at the community level. Thus the nation-state became too small for the global problems and too large for the local ones.

That could be handled in various ways. However, the really serious aspect of the nation-state was its tendency to seek its security through building and maintaining military strength. Each nation was autonomous and resisted any thought of worldwide collaboration to maintain order on the planet. World War I brought the shocking realization that continuance of this state of affairs was going to be terribly costly. And with World War II, the point was emphasized still more strongly by introduction of mass obliteration of civilian populations through saturation bombing and nuclear weapons. Thus it should have become apparent that, from World War II on, *national and global security, in any meaningful sense of the term, can no longer be attained through military strength.* Mikhail Gorbachev so wrote in *Perestroika* in 1987. However, the history of politics over the past four decades has been largely a history of attempts to evade and deny that fact.

Something over a half century ago it was commonplace to hear talk of some future world government. Since then, people have become extremely wary of concentrations of power, because they tend to attract corruptible individuals. It seems that national and global security will have to be sought elsewhere than either military strength or world government. As of the beginning of the new decade little progress has been made, and highly armed nations and continued reliance on nuclear deterrence have made the world a permanently perilous place.

3. Government by interest group

In the absence of a compelling sense of national or supranational purpose to which all subscribe, politics becomes largely a matter of competing groups, each vying for its own self-interests. That the result lacks the coherent sense of purpose necessary to solve the world's vexing problems should not be surprising.

The United States had, through most of its history, a strong sense of national purpose and overarching goals; the 1988 presidential campaign and succeeding events furnish ample evidence that whatever of this remains is very weak indeed. In the developing European Community one sees the beginning, perhaps, of overarching goals that go beyond economic and political power. Surely the shift from separate and competing nations to a sense of common European destiny is in itself a revolutionary step.

If fragmentation and lack of overarching goals is characteristic of present-day United States and European society, the same is all the more true at the global level. Although the United Nations has development and environment programs, there is no agreement on what development is good for people and for the planet, and no agreement on what system change will be required to halt the disastrous environmental and climate-change consequences of the world economy's carrying on "business as usual." Although the nations of the world have agreed in principle to the U.N.'s Universal Declaration of Human Rights, the guaranteeing of which could suffice as a worthy overarching global goal, there is no agreement on what to do when the normal practices of nations and the world economy systematically infringe upon those rights.

4. Predominance of materialistic picture of reality

It is apparent that a good formula for disaster is to attempt to make decisions affecting the future of a person, a society, or the planet, based on a perception of reality that isn't true. Many persons in recent years have been shocked at realizing that is precisely what modern society has been attempting to do.

The development of modern science was one of the great evolutionary leaps in the history of human societies. It was the democratization of knowledge, as well as the evolution of a set of highly effective techniques for gaining new knowledge of a certain sort. The scientific spirit was a new spirit of open inquiry, and public validation of knowledge. No longer was knowledge to be the property of a priesthood or power elite; anyone interested was invited to perform the experiments, and validate knowledge for himself or herself.

For a long time few noticed that the new scientific knowledge had a bias, which over several centuries began to have serious consequences. The bias was simply that it focused on the world of outer experience and neglected the world of *inner* experience. Closely related to that was the fact that it explained phenomena in terms of physical causation, neglecting that in our experience we find that there is also *volitional* causality; that is, human decisions causing things to happen. There were good reasons for that bias at the time empirical science was first being developed; it was highly advantageous in terms of a strong and effective science.

Nevertheless, one of the consequences of such a science—which seemed to be making an increasingly strong case for a materialistic worldview and random evolution of life forms, including us—was the erosion of the religious base underlying the values of Western civilization. As that base became weaker, particularly among those with the most education, the values became weaker. Manipulative rationality and acquisitive materialism became the hallmarks of "advanced" societies. But they are inadequate values, and the materialistic worldview is an inadequate worldview on which to make the kinds of decisions the future requires.

In Chapters 3 and 4 we will examine more thoroughly how the value-insensitive materialism which had been becoming stronger and stronger until the mid-1960s now seems to be giving way to a new recognition that we are, after all, spiritual beings in a spiritual universe, and how that recognition causes no conflict with a mature science.

The predominance of a materialistic worldview and the accompanying weakness of value and meaning commitments has led to what is probably the deepest-level problem of all—alienation. We are alienated from nature, of which we are a part and upon which we utterly depend. As a result, we foul our own nest and threaten the Earth's life-support systems necessary for our prospering and, in the end, for our survival. We are alienated from our work, since that has in so many cases become devoid of meaning. We are alienated from each other, since the sense of joint commitment to any transcendent goals is so weak. And, being deeply confused about our own being, we are alienated from ourselves.

That is not a pessimistic observation. It is simply an indication of where we must start, as we seek to find our way out of the present predicament.

Chapter 3

Threads of a
New Social Fabric

Western culture shows impressive signs of weaving a new pattern. The warp of the new fabric is a host of social movements and voluntary groups that have appeared on both the American and international scenes urging cultural change in response to worrisome environmental, social, political, economic and personal crises. Over the last half century a tremendous number of visionary thinkers, intellectual reformers, academic analysts, social critics, and varied groups of ordinary people have called for changes in the basic social order.

These individuals and groups have approached the problems from different perspectives depending on their assessment of the underlying causes. In general they can be considered in three different categories:

1. Those who see the problems as arising from defective social organization and institutional structures, and hence seek *new ways of organizing the human enterprise;*
2. Those who find the origins of the problems in faulty relationships—between men and women, racial or ethnic groups, social and economic classes, nation-states, and even between humans and other creatures and the Earth itself—and hence urge *new ways of relating;* and finally,
3. Those who perceive the problems to be rooted in the essential or conditioned nature of human beings, and so call for *new ways of being.*

Although it has seemed convenient to organize the discussion below in terms of these three categories, clearly they are not definitive and distinct; they overlap and bear similar themes. Each example in any of the three categories, for instance, implies questions about the fundamental nature of human beings, the exercise of power, and the locus of authority. Each response contributes insights that represent a powerful challenge to Western culture and which, taken as a whole, prefigure a new world in the making.

New Ways of Organizing the Human Enterprise

A growing pressure to restructure some of society's major institutions—the family, business, science and technology, the nation-state system, and religion—has been evident for at least a century. Nineteenth-century elements of this force included the abolitionist, labor, women's suffrage, socialist, populist, religious liberalism, and colonial independence movements. These various groups challenged traditional institutional forms, rallying around such basic value concepts as human dignity, intellectual and political freedom, fairness and justice.

The contemporary form of this pressure comprises similar elements, and some new ones. We examine the most important of these below.

Restructuring security; working for peace. No institution has threatened our very existence as much as has reliance on legitimated violence to settle international conflict. For most of the period since World War I there has been some sort of an active movement calling for an end to war and armed conflict. But the world has been slow to recognize (as noted in Chapter 2) that the concept of national security through military strength is obsolete. People have gradually been recognizing the inadequacy of a concept of security which (a) is based on capacity to destroy, and (b) ignores massive environmental destruction, the hazards of staggering debt, and the persistence of major concentrations of hunger and poverty.

Such traditional peace groups as the Quakers, and the nonviolent anti-war movement which grew out of the civil rights movement of the 1960s, have been joined in recent years by a legion of newer disarmament and multi-issue groups—Beyond War, Sane/Freeze, Women Against Nuclear Destruction, Physicians for Social Responsibility, International Physicians for the Prevention of Nuclear War, Mobilization for Survival, Jobs for Peace, to name just a few— to educate and lobby for a reduction of violence and a redefinition of peace in the modern world. The contemporary peace movement has many more dimensions than the highly visible demonstrations against nuclear weapons deployments. These include citizen diplomacy, solidarity with the Third World, human services coalitions, economic conversion efforts, and recent articulations of "organic" security.

The "citizen diplomacy" activities that arose in the 1980s were a response to frustration with governments. Groups of ordinary citizens decided that international peace and global security are no longer something to be left to diplomats and technical experts. The thousands of Americans who traveled to the Soviet Union in the 1980s offering person-to-person friendship, and the hundreds who went to Nicaragua to offer unofficial help, were truly "citizen diplomats" who took matters into their own hands when the professionals failed to break down barriers and establish peaceful relationships between countries.

Solidarity with the Third World is one component of contemporary "Green" thinking in Europe and elsewhere. For example, numerous organizations have arisen during the last decade to resist U.S. policies in Central America, particularly in Nicaragua and El Salvador. They focus on the oppression suffered by the ordinary people of Latin America, arising from economic structures and policies that have the effect of benefiting the already privileged, sustaining economic inequities, and inhibiting democratic processes.

Other groups are publicizing the disparity between military expenditures and the far lesser amounts made available for human services such as health care, aid for the homeless, child care for working mothers, and assistance to low-income families. Still others are working with communities to help them reduce dependence on defense-related spending, and to search for ways to convert jobs and technology to peaceful production. Still another perspective is that of "organic" security. This approach takes in human and ecological issues along with security, broadly defined, under a far more inclusive banner than "national security."

The various efforts to take a more basic approach to national and global security have stimulated a questioning of other underlying assumptions which end up supporting institutionalized violence—the sorts of violence that are imposed on people who lack adequate food, clothing, shelter, or economic opportunity. "Structural violence," a term coined by Norwegian peace researcher Johan Galtung, is meant to connote the deleterious impact on people from inequities built into societal patterns and institutions. It manifests in many ways, including poverty, homelessness, ghetto housing, unemployment, racial discrimination, factory closures, labor exploitation, oppressive sexist social patterns, demeaning welfare programs, economic imperialism, all of which do violence to the people involved because of their intrinsic inequity. Pope John XXIII summarized it: "If you want peace, work for justice."

Restructuring economics. The many forms of structural violence are directly related to the organization of economic life, and Pope John's dictum was surely meant to apply here. In fact, religious organizations have been among the most persistent critics of Western industrialism and its life-as-consumer ethic. Since the founding of the United States there has been a persistent minority, beginning with the Puritan colonists, who have insisted that the health of the whole community was more important than the opportunity for any one individual to become rich. Jonathan Winthrop's oft-quoted sermon to the Massachusetts colony summed it up: "We must delight in each other, make each other's conditions our own, rejoice together, mourn together, labor and suffer together, always having before our eyes our community as members of the same body." His description clearly assumes a different model of community and individual relationships, and a different institutional framework, from that of our current production/consumption-focused economy.

Such a new model was put forth by E.F. Schumacher in the 1970s. His thinking about alternative economics was pioneering, and clearly a harbinger of much of today's most innovative thinking. Basically a call for the restructuring of economics and attitudes about the role of work in human life, *Small is Beautiful: Economics as if People Mattered* (1973) ventured to suggest that the Buddhist concept of "right livelihood" might have relevance also in the West; that the placing of spiritual health as a goal to be sought along with material well-being deserves more attention than conventional economics would seem to suggest. Whereas conventional economics describes work as a "disutility"—something to be avoided, mechanized, and ideally eliminated—Schumacher reaffirmed an idea inherent in many religious traditions, that vocation or "right livelihood" has a central role in spiritual health.

In *Good Work* (1979) Schumacher summarized the objectionable characteristics of modern industrial society:

1. Its vastly complicated nature which tends to disempower the individual;

2. Its continuous stimulation of, and reliance on, the motivations of greed, envy, and avarice;
3. Its destruction of the content and dignity of most forms of work;
4. Its authoritarian character, owing to organization in excessively large units.

Much of the thrust of the "alternative economics" movement is to correct these characteristics. (Daly, 1977; Henderson, 1988; Lutz, 1979) A key element in this thinking is the role of technology.

Moving toward more appropriate technology. The public has shown a steadily increasing awareness of the consequences of indiscriminate technological advance. Much of the alienation reported in modern society is linked to technology; work satisfaction, environmental problems, health concerns, and reproductive freedom are all linked to technology and its use. More subtle are the many ways in which the technological choices both result from and sustain the patriarchal societal patterns already noted.

Growing concerns in the late 1960s produced a call for "technology assessment," which resulted in creation of the Office of Technology Assessment in the Federal Government. The basic idea was that we have to look ahead, and when a technological application is proposed, an assessment of its long-range impacts should be made. The political process, it was hoped, would then be wise enough to decide whether or not to develop and apply the technology.

Unfortunately, the forces pushing for application have often proved to be too strong for the orderly political process to stop any major projects once they achieved momentum. Only when *people* were sufficiently aroused, as in the case of the nuclear power industry— where the issues were highlighted by frightening accidents—was the story otherwise. The problem is that there are too many subtle driving forces that come into play. Many would concur with Langdon Winner's observation (1977) that technology has become autonomous, "that somehow technology has gotten out of control and follows its own course, independent of human direction." Some diagnose Western society as addicted to technology and technique. (Schaef, 1987)

Part of the trouble lies in the long-standing disjunction between science and technology on the one hand, and morality and values on the other—the "Two Cultures" which C.P. Snow deplored a half century ago. This split segregated the questions of "How to do it?" and "What should be done?", allowing the extension of power over nature to be regarded as value-free and morally unquestionable. But there are other potent historical, economic, and psychological forces that act to make it very difficult to reassess a technological development once underway. In general, if a technological application will make profit for somebody, or contribute to big weaponry or big medicine, there is a powerful tendency to develop and apply it— regardless of the possible negative consequences it may have for some groups of people, for future generations, or for the ecological systems of the Earth.

Thus it falls to the public, to concerned citizens, to ask the difficult questions and to act, if necessary, to delegitimate and halt the offending technologies. Does this new tool, power source, or technique serve to unduly concentrate political or economic power? Will it, if adopted, distort social priorities? Will it encourage further urbanization; bureaucratization; alienation? Does it compromise professional ethics? Would it foster or hinder greater economic and social equity among different groups in society, and among nations? Would it make us more secure, or more vulnerable? Does it introduce major economic, environmental, or social risks? Would it nurture or require an elitist technocracy that might further erode the democratic process?

By the 1970s the "appropriate technology" movement had begun to ask these questions. "Appropriate technology," E.F. Schumacher wrote in 1973, "is technology that is consciously developed and applied, driven by the highest values of the society, incorporating awareness of the needs of women and the demands of the environment, simple, approachable, life-enhancing and 'convivial,' and 'human-scale.'" Kirkpatrick Sale (1980; p. 157) defined it thus:

> A human-scale technology would need to be designed according to human needs, human capabilities and human forms.... It would have to be prosthetic—that is, created with human ends in mind—rather than cybernetic—that is, created largely with mechanical or technological ends in mind.... It would take form at a scale sufficiently small so that an individual could control it, sufficiently simple so that an individual could comprehend it, and sufficiently approachable so that an individual could fix it.... And it would enhance the human users rather than alienate them, make them feel good rather than exploited, satisfy rather than frustrate the innate human desire for accomplishment and achievement.

The choice for appropriate technology is guided by humane values. Present technology decisions are predominantly influenced by economic rationality, and consequently often end up being less than "appropriate."

The new way of business. Many changes are taking place within the corporation, centering around the individual. Survey data as well as less formal observation makes it clear that the traditional motivators for job performance—job security, high pay, and good benefits—no longer work. Employees want such intangibles as being treated with respect, having work that is personally satisfying, having ample opportunity to learn new skills and to grow personally, having a reasonable amount of autonomy, being recognized for good work. John Naisbitt's study of trends among workers (1985), as well as the more recent study by Michael Maccoby (1988), note the increasingly widespread idea that work should be both economically rewarding and emotionally fulfilling.

As impractically idealistic as it might have seemed to a previous generation of managers, the new view is that *workers can manage themselves.* As Naisbitt puts it (1985; p. 96), corporate America is coming to a new "ideal of the model employee.... We are shifting the ideal... from one who carries out orders correctly to one who takes responsibility and initiative, monitors his or her own work, and uses managers and supervisors in their new roles as facilitators, teachers, and consultants."

Workers are insisting on, and increasingly receiving, recognition as *stakeholders* in the enterprise, with rights of participation commensurate with their responsibilities. This is a step toward challenging the legitimacy of the time-honored concept that the shareholders, with their typically short-term view exclusively focused on stock earnings, should so heavily influence management decisions. As some have put it, "The employees are investing their lives; the shareholders are only investing money."

A further development in workplace reorganization is the growing popularity of worker-owned organizations, from the Employee Stock Option Plans (ESOP) in which the workers become part owners by virtue of acquiring stock in the company, to the worker-owned-and-managed Mondragon cooperatives in the Basque region of Spain. (The fact that ESOPs have sometimes been used by management primarily to ward off a potential hostile takeover points up that it is not in specific devices that salvation lies, but rather in deep-level change.)

Indeed, Terry Mollner (1990) identifies the Mondragon cooperatives as the prototype of "the third way...what we will be doing when we are not doing capitalism and socialism anymore." As relationships become more important than materialistic concerns, as wholeness and oneness replace separateness and competition, the issues of political left and right become unimportant, and the way is opened for a new, more cooperative and familial kind of organization to become the norm.

Toward a new development. Signs of this growing concern for a new economics are evident, not only within the industrialized countries, but in the developing countries as well. Travel and communication have breached the barriers that distance and cultural difference once maintained, and a global community exists in a sense never before experienced by the human race. Such institutions as the World Bank, the International Monetary Fund, the United Nations Development Programme, and numerous other international groups link the world economically; virtually no country in the world is economically isolated, or out of the global trading network. Business is now global: Research, design, fabrication, assembly, and marketing are now a global operation. Similarly, issues that might once have been the concerns of individual developing countries now have global significance.

Everywhere, people have begun to question the long-term viability of our present economic arrangements. The call for a restructuring of the global economy comes from many groups in the developed countries, including environmentalists, human rights groups, feminists, and economists such as Herman Daly, E.F. Schumacher, Hazel Henderson, and Mark Lutz focusing on alternatives—as well as elements of business. Business, in fact, has financed a number of the commissioned studies that have questioned the long-term viability of present economic practices and institutions: *The Limits to Growth, Reshaping the International Order, Mankind at the Turning Point.* A number of national governments have issued analyses similar to the United States' Global 2000 report. The Brundtland Commission Report *Our Common Future* (World Commission on Environment and Development, 1987) summarizes much of what had appeared before. It minces no words in its call for "sustainable development," pointing out the necessity for major structural reform in the economy:

> The pursuit of sustainability requires major changes in international economic relations.... Two conditions must be

satisfied.... The sustainability of ecosystems on which the global economy depends must be guaranteed. And the economic partners must be satisfied that the basis of exchange is equitable; relationships that are unequal and based on dominance of one kind or another are not a sound and durable basis for interdependence. (p. 67)

The developing countries too have been articulate on the matter, although their emphases have been, understandably, somewhat different. In 1974, at a special session of the United Nations on economic issues, the Third World caucus (Group of 77) began a campaign for a "New International Economic Order" (NIEO). Having achieved political decolonization, the developing countries of Africa, Asia, and Latin America found that they were still economically dependent. In their view, the advanced industrialized nations' control of world trade and finance left much of the Third World impoverished. The Northern countries tended to resent what seemed to them to be assaults on the normal conduct of commerce and finance. With the NIEO demands coming shortly after the power of OPEC to set high oil prices had been so disturbingly demonstrated, the North regarded them as an attempt to dictate the conduct of international trade and finance.

In the years since, indications have multiplied that the problem has many dimensions beyond the economic. Deeper understanding of the origins, and of the fuller implications of the Third World debt crisis, makes it clear that what is at stake is the right of other cultures, not congruent with the culture and values which are implicit in the one-world economy, to survive on the planet.

Partly as a consequence of this new understanding, the specific demands for a NIEO have become less strident. In light of the increasingly desperate situation of some of the countries, and in reaction to a sense of frustration, the leaders of the coalition of developing countries backed away somewhat from the broad cause of the NIEO and put their emphasis on such more specific and urgent issues as debt relief and the policies and operative procedures of the World Bank and the International Monetary Fund. At the same time, there is evident, in capitalist, socialist, and developing countries alike, a growing recognition that the global exigencies will require in the longer term a major restructuring of the world economy.

The central focus of this thinking, which is typified to some extent by the Brundtland Commission Report, is the puzzle of *global development.* The ultimate goal of development, implicit in the concept of development that dominated during the two decades following World War II, was a high-consumption Western industrial monoculture spread around the globe. It is now almost unanimously agreed that "success" by that measure, even if it were feasible, is not viable from the standpoints of environment and resources. A continuation of present trends, on the other hand, appears to lead to a teeming and impoverished South, and a sated, over-consuming North (with its own marginalized subgroups—the homeless, the chronically unemployed, and a growing underclass). That is a future full of injustice, conflict, and peril. What, then, comprises a satisfactory path to the global future?

Elements that appear in the dialogue on this topic include:

- *Sustainability as a central guidepost;* just as the oldtime farmer tried to leave the land better than he found it, so the new world economy needs to leave the planet, its major ecological and life-support systems, each decade in at least as good shape as the decade before.
- A *"land ethic"* more or less as proposed by ecologist Aldo Leopold (1966), which acknowledges the rights of natural systems.
- *National and global accounting systems* that incorporate health-related factors, environmental costs, protection of natural beauty, impacts on the well-being of future generations and non-human living creatures, and other non-economic variables into guidance procedures for technology implementation and other major decisions.
- Emphasis on development and application of *appropriate technology* as defined above.
- Emphasis on a *socially constructive role for business,* beyond the economic.
- Emphasis on *work as vocation,* as a central and fulfilling aspects of one's life.
- Balance of economic and *social justice* objectives.

Restructuring to eliminate patriarchal bias. The thousands of years of patriarchal influence on modern culture was reviewed earlier. As the women's movement has been influenced by growing consciousness of the central importance of this historical shaping, its potentiality to be a force for profound social change has increased.

The women's movement is a general awakening and asserting of the value of the feminine, in men as well as in women. As C.G. Jung said many decades ago, as men recognize and free this suppressed part of themselves they become more whole, and life becomes more rich. It is not that the differences between the genders disappear; rather in the process of discovering the other half of oneself the differences become more appreciated and more exciting.

In general, the feminine way is to feel oneself to be intimately a part of the surrounding world, and to regard power not as "power over" someone, but as a quality innate in each individual, available for creative purposes, potentially in limitless supply. It is quite alien to the feminine side to try to control and dominate the universe, or to be obsessed with demonstrating "power over nature." The feminine way is to view leadership as facilitation and nurturing, rather than control or direction. Its approach to work and life tends to be more process-oriented than product-oriented; in relating to others it starts from a position of parity, assuming the other to be an equal. The feminine way is more cooperative than competitive; it involves trust in intuition, and thinking that is holistic, multivariant and multidimensional. Most importantly, "knowing" tends to be a *relational* thing, an ongoing process between an individual and other persons, nature, a "higher Self"—instead of a process of intellectual abstraction.

Women's influence is perceptible in current tendencies to break away from patterns of domination by experts and authorities, to move toward cooperation over competition, to break down the rigid divisions between management and labor, to challenge the notion in science that reductionism is the way to understand things, to oppose militarism, to resist manipulative technologies.

If there is increasing awareness of the price exacted in the past by the patriarchal organization of society, and an already observable decline in its hold, one naturally asks: What will replace it? The answer would seem to be neither matriarchy nor some gender-neutral form of external power, but rather a devolution of power to the local level—ultimately, to within the individual. This devolution is supported by a number of trends in the overall pattern of social movements:

- Decentralization of power from higher to lower levels.
- Return to human scale in structuring.
- Resurgence of localism.
- De-bureaucratization.
- Worker self-management and humanization of the workplace.
- Focus on self-help and the development of new individual ways of being.

The basic reason is that the "feminine" values that are being newly appreciated—emphasizing relationships to life forces, one another, and inner spirit—are fostered best in small face-to-face groupings like family, community, and the small work group.

Restructuring government. The desirability of decentralization of government and of the devolution of power is implicit in "new age politics." (Satin, 1979; Sale, 1980) But it is not simply decentralization: What is required by the nature of the global dilemmas is localization of the approaches to some problems, and globalization of others. A number of developments over the past quarter century suggest that this is not such an improbable goal as a first glance might suggest.

At one extreme, we see the appearance, all over the globe, of groups within nations agitating for separatism or partial autonomy: the Baltic States, the Basques in Spain, the Québecois in Canada, the Welsh in Britain, the Native American and Australian Aborigine indigenous peoples, and many others throughout the world. In developing countries a recurrent theme is recognition that "alternative development"—focusing on the development of people, strengthening self-reliance, and building on native cultural roots—implies autonomy at the local level. Similarly, the welfare programs that work are those that help people help themselves in local arenas.

History has repeatedly shown that when central governments fail, local citizen groups, spontaneous organs of government as it were, rise up to meet the need for coordination and direction. The tradition of the New England 'town meeting' shows both the vitality that such local governments can have, and also the tenacity with which local traditions can be defended in the face of national-government attempts to encroach on local prerogatives.

At the other extreme, we see the rise of transnational groups formed to address global issues at a level above the national. Some of these, such as the World Bank, the International Monetary Fund, and the International Court of Justice, are spawned by the United Nations; others, the "non-governmental organizations" (NGOs) in United Nations parlance, arose from private-sector or grassroots initiatives. These "NGOs" include, among hundreds of others, the International Institute for Environment and Development, Worldwatch Institute, and the International Red Cross. *More of the required transnational structure for dealing with global concerns is in place than is generally appreciated.*

Alternatives to bureaucracy. Criticisms of bureaucracy, in both public and private sectors, are well represented in the current critiques of modern society. Bureaucracies tend to put a premium on conformity, "scientific" rationality, efficiency, expertise, certitude, and control. They stifle creativity and innovation; they sanction responsibility without accountability. They tend to create "structural violence" and "co-dependence." Often, personal relationship is devalued in bureaucracies; people tend to be valued for how they play certain roles, rather than as human beings. Workers are termed "human resources"; when a corporate "takeover" occurs, the "human resources" are passed on to the new owners and managers, reminiscent of the way chattel slaves used to be passed from owner to owner.

As a consequence of these shortcomings of bureaucracy, many persons seek to become associated with organizations that foster freedom and opportunity for personal growth, empowerment, and environmental rehabilitation; cooperation and mutual aid among the members of society; and the creation of systems of interaction that will be viable in the long-term future. These characteristics are most likely to be found in "human-scale" organizations in which there is a great deal of personal autonomy, with individual actions coordinated through shared vision (as with the "metanoic" organization described by Charles Kiefer in Adams (1984; pp. 69-84). Such organizations take into account the new motivations of workers, and the new definitions they are giving to work and life goals.

Interwoven in all these pressures to restructure institutions is a *change in the locus of authority*. This shift, from external authority (e.g. the Church, moral and ethical rules, the Expert) to internal authority (trust in oneself), has been accelerating over the past several decades. It has already impacted all the other signs of change we have been considering. It is manifesting all over the globe, in the rising democratization and liberation movements; in feminist challenges to patriarchy; in new spiritual movements calling into question traditional religious systems and formulations.

Expanding assurance of human rights. Much progress has been made over the past two centuries in expanding the assurance of human rights to all groups. The concept of the global village calls all planetary citizens to seek an end to arbitrary divisions and labels: North and South, East and West, Communist and "free", etc. It invites us to relate to other peoples in such ways that there can no longer be accusations of "economic imperialism"; to recognize our shared humanity, common goals, needs and hopes; to work to lessen the barriers of language and prejudice, even as we celebrate our diversity of cultures, lifestyles, and ways of being and doing. In furtherance of this mission, the General Assembly of the United Nations adopted, in 1948, a Universal Declaration of Human Rights. Under this Declaration and the Covenants that make it legally binding, for the first time in history, responsibility for the protection and pursuit of human rights is assumed by the international community and accepted as a permanent obligation. Still there is much to be done.

Within individual countries the picture is a little brighter. After a civil war and three Constitutional amendments, the U.S., in 1865, eliminated slavery as an institution and assured the civil rights of blacks; still, it took another century to recognize and begin to eliminate the many remaining blocks to full equality for blacks. The activism of groups such as the Students' Nonviolence Coordinating Committee, the NAACP, CORE, and the Urban League, both manifested and contributed to the deepening ethical commitment to racial equality in the United States. Even so, there are still manifold subtle ways in which racial discrimination remains, even though it is no longer acceptable in its overt form.

Women's rights have been closely connected to the issue of the civil rights of nonwhites. Under English common law women had no right to own property and no legal entity or existence apart from their husbands. In the United States women were given equal voting rights with men through passage of the 19th Amendment in 1920; they attained the same status in Great Britain in 1928. Many who had enlisted in the cause of women's suffrage anticipated that women's voting would transform the American body politic. When this failed to happen during the "Roaring Twenties," the women's movement as a focused political entity became splintered and disorganized, not to be reborn until the mid-1960s. By the 1980s many men were taking up the women's cause, recognizing that men as well as women needed to be liberated from the sexism of the past. The women's movement is no longer solely or even primarily about equal rights for women; it is also about reducing long-standing patriarchal institutional forms, and about a major shift of value emphasis away from the hierarchy and fragmentation characteristic of patriarchal society, toward a balance that will be more wholesome for women and men.

Slowly, over the last few decades, awareness has been rising about the need for ethical protections for such vulnerable groups as children, the handicapped, the mentally ill and comatose, prisoners, and now those suffering from AIDS. One of these movements representing those unable to speak for themselves is that concerned with animal rights; it seems clearly to be gaining in strength.

This growing concern for how structures infringe on human rights is an aspect of how we relate to one another.

"Green thinking." Most of these aspects of restructuring are included in the "Green thinking" which is growing stronger, not only in Europe but throughout the developed world. (We are distinguishing "Green thinking" from the "Green" political organizations that exist in around 20 countries. The latter are a political force whose importance varies with time and place. The underlying thinking is far more durable and ubiquitous.)

Diana Schumacher lists as the key elements of "Green thinking": alternative economics; holistic health care; conservation; organic agriculture; animal rights; solidarity with the Third World; a non-nuclear future; renewable energy sources; meaningful work; small, appropriate technology; care for the rights of minorities; self-reliance; local self-sustainability; and peaceful actions toward transition.

New Ways of Relating

A significant component of "new paradigm" thinking and contemporary social movements perceives the origins of our problems to be in faulty relationship patterns, some of which are thousands of years old.

From domination to partnership. Liberation from domination is one of the major thrusts of new-relationship thinking. Domination by rich over poor, powerful over weak, has been a perennial problem through history—both within the society and between nations. Domination has sometimes been through force and political structures, sometimes through control of economic factors; sometimes more covertly through psychological pressures. The concept of economic rights was slower to develop than that of civil rights, not really gaining strength until the socialist movements of the late nineteenth century. In the last two decades it has become clear that welfare programs for the poor and "development aid" programs for the poor countries can be but a subtler form of domination. Thus liberation involves empowerment of the poor and weak through removal of structural forms of domination, as well as increased autonomous effort by people on their own behalf.

Domination in modern society is often less overt than a generation or more ago, but nonetheless powerful. Paternal domination, openly acceptable in much of European and American culture until recent generations, is far less so now, and yet it persists (along with maternal manipulation) in a more subtle form. Liberation from domination is an important aspect of the women's movement and children's rights movement.

Society's definition of "normal" is a part of the pattern of domination over those who, in whatever way, deviate from the norm—whether through physical or mental handicap, skin color, gender, or whatever. Although ethnic and class domination remains a ubiquitous factor in practically all societies, liberation from this domination remains an essential goal of the civil rights movement.

We can also be dominated by a lifestyle to which we have become accustomed. This is a theme in the "voluntary simplicity" movement, reflecting the feeling

> ... that we have lost touch with a deeper, more profound part of our beings.... We long for a simpler way of life that allows us to restore some balance to our lives.... There are many who have already begun the search for a more conscious balance, a simplicity of living that allows the integration of inner and outer, material and spiritual.... The exploration of new ways of living that support new ways of being is a movement that arises from the awakening of compassion ... the dawning realization that the fate of the individual is intimately connected with the fate of the whole.... [The affluent] must learn the difference between those material circumstances that support our lives and those that constrict our lives. Simplicity requires living with balance.... To find such balance ... requires that we understand the difference between our personal 'needs' and our 'wants'... each person [must consider] whether his or her level and pattern of consumption fits with grace and integrity into the practical art of daily living on this planet. (Elgin, 1981; pp. 165-8)

Relating to nature. The environmental crisis has awakened us to what may be the most fundamental form of domination, that of nature by human beings. After decades of thoughtless plunder of the Earth's resources and reckless pollution of air, water, and soil, awareness is now widespread that something must be done. People are gradually realizing that humans can not own a portion of the Earth, that real estate can never be a form of property in the sense of being a "thing" upon which, as owner, one can commit any manner of destruction. The Earth is the substructure for the natural support systems on which all life depends; a web of ecosystems, the disturbance of which one should undertake only with great caution; a "resource" that belongs equally to all living beings.

Numbers of activists have spoken up over the past half century decrying the violence of ecosystem destruction. Many more have urged the need to do something about pollution and, recently, changes in climate and depletion of the ozone layer. Others have stressed the spirit-renewing value of pristine wilderness. Individuals and organizations have responded to the call, and much restoration is under way.

Yet the main thing learned through all of this is that what can be achieved through direct action toward environmental protection is limited. Changes have to take place at two other levels, at least. One is a genuine change in the way we perceive our relationship to the natural world including the other creatures on the planet. The other is a major change in the institutionalized incentives that influence us to pollute and destroy natural habitat. Both are happening, although by no means as fast as the situation warrants.

Harmonizing with, rather than dominating over, nature is not a new idea: It is still a central part of the cultures of the indigenous tribes almost everywhere in the world that they yet survive. The awareness of our intimate connectedness to nature that informs the modern ecological movement was innate with the natives who originally inhabited North America; the same was not always true for European civilization, or with the Europeans who emigrated to the New World. Thus the conservationist and the preservationist (wilderness) movements of the nineteenth and twentieth centuries found themselves strongly at odds with commercial and some government interests. A good part of the problem is that, as one of the pioneers of the ecological movement, Aldo Leopold, said (1966; pp. 238-240):

> There is as yet no ethic dealing with man's relation to land and to the animals and plants that grow upon it.... [Such] a 'land ethic' changes the role of *Homo sapiens* from conqueror of the land-community to plain member and citizen of it. It implies respect for his fellow-members, and also respect for the community as such.... No important change in ethics was ever accomplished without an internal change in our intellectual emphases, loyalties, affections and convictions.

In other words, a profound shift is required in the way we perceive our relatedness. This is coming about through forces from several different directions. One impetus is simply the logical necessity of a change in attitude in order that the environment may continue to support human habitation.

Other forces include the shifts in values implicit in the respiritualization movement and the feminist movement. One of the more important thrusts in this direction comes from the combination of a renewal of pride in their indigenous culture on the part of the Native North American Indians, and the humble realization on the part of a growing percentage of "whites" that the Indian culture might have something valuable to offer them. In the Indian's perception the universe is all of a piece—with no separation between man and nature, or spirit and body. All of the universe is alive, and all of the creatures in it are our relatives. We are simply enjoined to behave accordingly.

A growing number of thoughtful persons are re-interpreting Christianity to substitute stewardship for the traditional "dominion" over creation. They are coming to realize "the interdependence of all living forms on Earth, they are developing a new 'spirituality of the Earth,' a 'creation spirituality' whereby they recognize and celebrate the gift of life animating the Earth, and they acknowledge and venerate its sacredness." (King, 1989; p. 95) "Creation-centered spirituality" as articulated by Catholic theologian Matthew Fox is insistent on the sacredness of the natural world. A similar call comes from the "deep ecology" movement: "More than just reform is needed. Many philosophers and theologians are calling for a new ecological philosophy for our time. We believe, however, that we may not need something new, but need to reawaken something very old, to reawaken our understanding of Earth wisdom." (Devall and Sessions, 1985; p. ix) This "deep ecology" approach requires retrieving that "participating consciousness" which would be so natural to us had we grown up in one of the indigenous cultures such as that of the Native American Indian. It requires an awareness of the radical relatedness of all life.

Kenneth Boulding epitomized the issue of our relationship to the Earth by contrasting what he called the "cowboy economy" of the past and the "spaceman economy" we must move to (1970; pp. 96-7):

> [I call] the open economy the 'cowboy economy,' the cowboy
> being symbolic of the illimitable plains and also associated with

reckless, exploitative, romantic and violent behavior, which is characteristic of open societies. The closed economy of the future might similarly be called the 'spaceman' economy, in which the Earth has become a single spaceship, without unlimited reservoirs of anything, either for extraction or for pollution, and in which, therefore, man must find his place in a cyclical ecological system which is capable of continuous reproduction of material form even though it cannot escape having inputs of energy.... In the cowboy economy, consumption is regarded as a good thing and production likewise;... the success of the economy is measured by the amount of the throughput from the 'factors of production.'... The gross national product is a rough measure of this total throughput.... By contrast, in the spaceman economy, throughput is by no means a desideratum, and indeed is regarded as something to be minimized rather than maximized.... What we are primarily concerned with is stock maintenance.... This idea that both production and consumption are bad things is very strange to economists.

Seven laws of ecology. It is in a way peculiar that economics and ecology should have come to be at odds with each other since they both stem from the same Greek root, *oikos*, "home" (as in home planet—Earth). Nearly twenty years ago an ecologist at Rutgers University, Bertram Murray, published an article in *The New York Times* with the title, "What the Ecologists Can Teach the Economists". (Murray, 1974) He argued that economics had, for nearly all of its history as an intellectual discipline, been operating and theorizing in ignorance or neglect of the laws of ecology—and hence gotten us into a sorry mess.

Seven laws of ecology, in particular, stand out as fundamental to a future restructuring of economics:

- *Everything is connected to everything else.* Economic decisions and policies cannot be made solely on the basis of optimizing some economic parameters, without taking into account politics, social situations, value considerations, and ecological realities.
- *There is no such thing as a free lunch.* In fact, as resources become more and more depleted and pollution grows, as options narrow and time frames shorten, lunch gets more and more expensive!
- *Nature knows best.* It takes considerable humility to recognize that human beings do not necessarily know all that needs to be known to manage an ecosystem. The ecological literature suggests that, because of this law, we should try to be tentative in our policies, and avoid courses of action that could commit

the Earth, or any major ecosystem, to a fate that might be irreparable.

- *Everything must go somewhere.* The waste-absorbing capability of the natural environment is already taxed to the point that recycling as a way of life is an inevitable choice.
- *Continuous growth leads to disasters.*

  The economic model of American businessmen, economists, and politicians demands continuously increasing growth.... Such continuous growth curves are not unknown in biological ... systems.... We call them cancer cells. Their growth is not indefinite. Indeed, they eventually kill the host organism.... In biological and physical systems, continuous growth [will eventually] lead to disasters. (Murray, 1974)

- *Competing species can not coexist indefinitely.* This is what the ecologists call the "competitive exclusion principle." It is a very different view of competition from that of the economists. While the economist feels competition is beneficial, serving to maintain diversity and stability, and providing the consumer with a wider array of choices, the ecologist realizes that, in a competitive situation in nature, one of the competing species will eventually be eliminated, either by being forced out of the ecosystem, or by being forced to use some other resource. Americans are reluctant to see this, but the facts of history suggest that competition in economic systems has the same effect as competition in ecosystems: It reduces the number of competitors.
- *The law of the retarding lead.* Studies of ecosystems in operation indicate that adaptive changes come not from the species dominant in their niche, but from species and individuals existing on the fringe and forced to be more resourceful. Applying this law in human and economic systems suggests that we might anticipate adaptive changes to be initiated, not by white males and the Fortune 500 companies, but by women, minorities, and small entrepreneurial firms.

Taken together, these seven laws suggest that the American economy (and, with minor qualifications, the economies of Europe and Japan), with its valuing of growth, waste, and competition, is inherently unstable. They imply limits to a technological approach to pollution control, and suggest that Americans are going to have to face the unpleasant fact of a declining material standard of living.

New ways of relating in the political arena. "New" or "Green" politics insists that central to the new way of handling power and operating governing systems is a commitment to change without violence. The commitment involves not only physical violence, but also structural violence (that is, institutionally built-in inequity). Thus concerns include social and economic restructuring: attending to the plight of the poor, homeless, abused, and addicted; strengthening and actively implementing civil rights legislation; extending ethical protection to include natural systems (Leopold's "land ethic" again); and, ending the patriarchal systems that block both women's and men's full development as persons and inflict upon the entire social system an unwholesome value bias. At the international level, concerns include developing non-exploitative economic institutions and trade relations, taking a stand against violence in international relations, and for education in peaceful means to resolve conflicts.

The "new " politics seeks to return to the participatory, human-scale democracy of ancient Greece but, obviously, including women, and substituting modern technologies for the Greek slaves. Its aims include more local involvement, grassroots initiatives, devolution of power, and a concern to work toward political processes that will be more responsive to the people. Recognizing the pluralistic nature of the American population, the new democracy will draw on the assets and strengths of its diversity of cultures, races and ethnic groups. Pluralism will come to be regarded as a great advantage, promoting adaptability, resourcefulness, and revitalization.

"Green" politicians advocate "soft energy paths" (energy conservation and use reduction; decentralized solar power); "appropriate," human-scale technologies, both in the industrialized and the developing countries; environmental rehabilitation; and regenerative agriculture (organic farming and gardening, decentralized and localized farming).

"Thinking globally, acting locally" is one of the mottoes of the new politics. We are all forced to a global awareness by a multitude of factors, including instantaneous global communications, jet plane speed of travel, the globalization of business, and environmental problems (e.g. acid rain, ocean pollution) that know no national borders. Holding a global perspective, and recognizing that the whole Earth is the ultimate ecological unit, on which we all depend for life, nevertheless we act primarily in a local and regional arena which is small enough in scale so that people do not feel disempowered, and feel they can affect outcomes; small enough for effective participatory democracy.

The value emphases informing the "new" politics are more balanced, and based in a more organic worldview, than those that have prevailed during the post-World War II period. The balance is between "soft," "feminine" nurturing, cooperative and caring values, and "masculine" competitive, aggressive values; between values of self-realization and holistic, ecological concern; between self-reliance and service for the well-being of the whole; between civil and human rights, and responsibilities and obligations as members of a community. The new worldview is holistic, life-affirming, and involves trust in an inner, intuitive wisdom. It tends to be eclectic in detail, but generally affirms the human need for far more than material well-being alone.

Living in community. The Latin word *communitas* referred to the sense of fellowship or feeling in community. A group in community comprises individuals who share common ties or interests, often through living in the same place and sharing ownerships or common similarities. A great many people find that the modern urban environment is not conducive to sustaining the sense of fellowship or commonality of interest that is the basis of true community. There have been many reactions to this in the form of "intentional communities," questing for community through returning to "human scale" settlements. While these attempts date back to the first half of the nineteenth century, they have been particularly prevalent since the 1960s. (Sale, 1980; Borsodi, 1948)

In addition to decentralization and the concern for "human scale," the next most important value in forming community is integration of work and life with the environment. The ideal communitarian society is typically described as bringing work back into an integrated relationship to self-governing living communities. For example, a residential group might collectivize its own resources to develop communal shopping, cooking, child care, cleaning, gardening and farming, small manufacturing, etc. The communalization of much of the equipment of daily life would drastically reduce the pattern of consumption, waste, and duplication of equipment in nuclear families. In a largely self-sustaining community with an ecological awareness, the amount of "waste" could be minimized.

Other, related values that accompany the desire for quality of life-in-community are nonviolence, "voluntary simplicity," self-sufficiency, and civic volunteering and spending on cultural, educational, and spirit-feeding activities.

A community of human scale is a place where participatory democracy is possible, each person able to see the need for his or her active role in the municipality, each individual's action having meaning and impact. Human scale makes easier the implementation of another key principle of the viable community: an economy at "steady state," minimizing throughput while maximizing the use of present stock, using techniques and industrial systems that minimize pollution and resource waste. (Daly, 1977; Schumacher, 1973)

One indicator of this yearning for community is that during the decades of the 1970s and 1980s hundreds of thousands of Americans moved from the cities to rural areas

> to reorder their lives in a new economic balance that often contains four elements:
> a) Producing goods (crops, furniture, house, clothing, etc.) to meet the needs and wants of one's own family;
> b) Producing goods or services that one sells (or barters) directly to other people for whatever currency is agreed on, rather than selling one's services to an institution;
> c) Investing money, thought, and effort in resources that reduce one's present or future need for money payout and consequent dependence on macrosystems (e.g. installing solar panels, wood stoves, windmills, etc.);
> d) Reducing to lifeline status one's connection to and participation in the professional or technical or administrative work that is executed for money (usually in an urban setting, usually for a large organization, usually in a knowledge-related form of activity.) (Schumacher, 1979; p. 196)

The evolving family. One of the more talked-about aspects of the 1960s was the breakdown of first the extended family and then the nuclear family—to be replaced by a variety of familial relationships arranged in other patterns. There were, as well, many changes in the relationships between partners—especially in the direction of more equality, freer expression of male feelings, and shared household duties. Fathers are also feeling freer to participate in childrearing, which benefits both parents and children.

Just as bureaucratic organizations manifest characteristics that promote addiction and co-dependency, so do family structures. Familiar role patterns include mutually clinging relationships; mutual deception patterns (e.g. having family "secrets" that no one acknowledges, such as physical or sexual abuse by the father, or someone's alcohol problem); making oneself indispensable to others; playing the martyr; needing to feel needed; needing to be in control of every situation; having distorted feelings (such as anger reflected as self-righteousness). There is nothing new in these patterns; what is new is that people are aware of and talking about them.

A key theme in the "new age" literature is "intentional living" which, in the context of the family, becomes "intentional parenting." Intentional parenting begins with realization of the sacrifices, time commitment and maturity that parenting entails. Another feature is planned (rather than accidental) conception, and good pre-natal care; this implicitly raises issues of eliminating the structural violence of poverty and poor schooling, and reducing the pressures from authoritarian structures that discourage women from exercising control over their reproductive lives.

To relate to the Earth with a changed consciousness; to relate in community with values like localism, feminism, cooperative nurturance, and economic equity; to relate to other creatures with an expanded ethical commitment; to work to eradicate the structural violence of sexism and to discover the masculine and feminine within each one of us; to create relationships of partnership rather than domination—all of these are facets of the "new relationships" thrust of contemporary change forces.

A New Way of Being

New ways of relating go hand in hand with new ways of being. Many people working for structural social change during the frenzied period of the 1960s experienced "burnout," broken relationships, substance addictions, conflicts between values and ideals and the realities of people's behavior. As a result, many of these people turned, as did a large number of the general public, to developing greater inner understanding, achieving new levels of personal well-being, seeking simpler and more harmonious ways to live, and searching for inner peace. Some journeyed to the East to explore non-Western spiritual traditions; others became involved with meditative disciplines and other forms of inner search. Thus political and social movements acquired a spiritual component, and the personal journey to self-realization took on more of a political and social component than ever before.

The "human potential" movement. The relationship between modern social movements and the discovery of the unconscious may not be immediately apparent; however, the links are so strong that some comprehension of the latter is essential to understanding the former. Sigmund Freud, more than anyone else, gave currency to the basic idea that the human mind has far more depth than ordinary, waking consciousness might suggest. Carl Jung broadened Freud's theories in a number of significant ways. In particular, his emphasis on the process of "individuation" laid important foundations for modern psychotherapies, and his concept of the "collective unconscious" has relevance both to individuals struggling to understand themselves, and to the growth and change of whole cultures adapting to challenging times.

Those who were endeavoring to achieve credibility for the youthful science of psychology found that the conceptual frameworks of clinical psychology and psychiatry were not sufficiently precise, and formulated a behaviorist psychology which restricted itself to that in human behavior which is measurable. By mid-twentieth century, behaviorism was the dominant approach in experimental psychology, and it was exerting influence in the clinical area as well. When this approach proved to be, in the eyes of an influential group of psychologists, sterile and offensive, a reaction gained ground in the late 1950s, resulting in "humanistic psychology." It was introduced as a "third force," complementing the existing psychiatric and behavioristic models already in place.

In helping individuals toward "self-actualization," humanistic psychologists were reconnecting with Western cultural roots—the humanist tradition of early Greece and Rome. Humanists like Rollo May, Abraham Maslow, and Carl Rogers reminded modern men and women of Western history's traditional emphasis on human dignity, freedom, liberty, rights and responsibilities, and on the vast potential that our humanity gives us as a birthright—an emphasis which behaviorism, with its more positivistic outlook, tended to ignore.

As a plethora of social movements kicked over the traces in the mid-1960s, humanistic psychologists saw their newly-formed discipline overrun with a wide variety of schools, theories, gurus, "new age" teachers, and cult figures pushing the borders of what it means to be human. There were *est* and Esalen; massage work and mantras; drug-experimentation, psychedelics, and psychic fairs— some of it sensible and insightful, some of it far less well grounded.

The human potential movement became a grab bag of the orthodox and unorthodox, legal and illegal, proven and untried. New ways of being were suggested, many were tried, and the answers provided by the old humanistic tradition were found too limiting. Thus "transpersonal psychology" was born.

The transpersonal response. Seeking to foster human development beyond the traditional views of humanism, transpersonal psychology arose in the 1970s. The ambiguous term "transpersonal" was chosen deliberately to invite an open-ended extension beyond the personal, including some dimensions that tended to be unacceptable to the orthodox scientific community. In the transpersonal view we are seen to limit ourselves and our capacities by our personal beliefs about reality and about ourselves. This is particularly true in the areas of mental functioning referred to by the terms "intuition" and "creativity." Whereas the psychoanalytic view introduced the concept of the subconscious mind, the transpersonal outlook stresses the presence, "above" the conscious mind, of a "supraconscious" or "higher self." (Vaughan and Walsh, 1980; Tart, 1975)

Self-help movements. From the mid-1960s on, the United States, and to a lesser extent Canada and northern Europe, saw a progressive disenchantment with the expert and the politician. From the shock with which the American people realized that President Eisenhower had lied to them about the U-2 incident, public attitudes shifted from near-absolute trust to total cynicism, where one hardly expected a high-ranking government official to tell the truth. So-called "experts" turned out to be woefully uninformed about the impact of their actions, especially, it seemed, where there was a possibility of environmental catastrophe. Physicians too were found wanting, their medical care assailed by feminists, cost-cutting bureaucrats, and biomedical ethicists. As a result of this disillusionment, people began to relearn the ability to take action on their own—to display a sense of self-reliance. This is another example of the shift from external to internal authority mentioned earlier.

The self-help movement was catalyzed by a spate of "how-to" books, workshops, programs, gurus, and renegade professionals, who helped people take charge of their own health, psychological, spiritual, and behavioral problems. In recent years the emphasis has shifted from physical, spiritual, psychological and intellectual regimens to a more specific focus on personal empowerment, ending addictions, creating new lives by changing limiting beliefs, and validating personal reality through inner authority.

Holistic health care. The holistic health movement, a primary development of the self-help movement, reflects a profound discontent with conventional or allopathic medicine. It is characterized by emphasis on:

- *Self-responsibility for physical well-being.* The individual, rather than relying on the doctor to patch him/her up, is responsible for actions to get well, stay well, and develop a set of personal habits that will foster health.
- *The practice of preventive medicine.* The holistic approach tends to stress the prevention of disease as much as integrated treatments when illness occurs.
- *The person as an integrated, interactive system* involving body, mind, and spirit.
- *The presence of an inner healer*—a part of the mind-body that "knows" how to help us grow, develop, heal, and fight off disease, and that is available for "consultation"—advice on treatment and future prevention.
- *Illness as opportunity*—opportunity to learn what habits, attitudes, beliefs may need changing.
- *An open-ended definition of health.* Being healthy involves not only being free of disease. To be healthy implies being robust, full of an energized sense of well-being, ease, vitality. It implies being integrated, at one with self and others, and with the total environment.

Group-help response to addiction and co-dependence. One particular aspect of the holistic health and self-help movements is achieving special importance. This is the group-help approach to problems of addiction, which has moved from being the most effective way to deal with alcoholism (Alcoholics Anonymous) to being a broad social movement in its own right.

A key component of the Alcoholics Anonymous approach to supporting the recovering alcoholic is the "twelve steps" program. These involve, first, admitting powerlessness over alcohol, and recognizing that life as an alcoholic had become unmanageable; recognizing the help possible from "a Power greater than myself" to aid in the restoration to sanity; taking moral inventory; admitting problems to others; trying to make amends to those persons harmed in the past; seeking contact with God "as we understand him"; and carrying the message of spiritual awakening to other alcoholics in a mutual support system.

This approach has proven so successful with alcoholism that it has been extended, over the past decade, to other forms of addiction—including all forms of chemical dependency, food abuse, gambling, sexual compulsions, and smoking. In addition, recognition of the mutual interdependence that occurs where a relationship involves addiction has led to the creation of support groups for spouses and children of alcoholics and other forms of co-dependence.

More recently, the ideas of addiction and co-dependence have been extended still further, to apply to the individual's relationships with organizations and society. (Schaef, 1987) Functioning as a closed system, and presenting the individual in it with few options in terms of roles and behaviors—or even ways of thinking and perceiving—the typical bureaucratic organization manifests dozens of patterns indicative of addiction. These include: vague, confused and indirect communication; written memos used to avoid face-to-face confrontations; secretive behavior; executive cover-up of real problems; avoidance of conflict and difficult issues; inability to tolerate "straight talk" and the honest expression of feelings. The corporate world, employees and executives alike, are rapidly awakening to the undesirability of this institutionalized co-dependence. Extending the concept of "addiction" in this way challenges us all to find new ways to live, work, and interact with others, in which we encourage one another to be free and mature, rather than to reinforce one another's imprisoning addictive patterns.

Personal responsibility and the locus of authority. A key aspect of the new way of being involves reperception of the locus of authority. The foundations for much of the Western concept of authority can be found in the hierarchical authoritarianism of Roman society. As Rome declined, the kind of authority represented in the hierarchical forms shifted from political to ecclesiastical. The infallibility of the Pope and the Divine Right of Kings illustrate the centralized nature of ultimate authority.

The 300 years from the late sixteenth to the late nineteenth century witnessed the rise to predominance of political forms of authority—nation-states, urban governments, and other forms of civil institutions claiming the right of coercive power over individuals. Despite the liberal-democratic tradition of *legitimate* authority by consent of the governed, there was in the latter part of this period a reaction from extreme liberals, who viewed the authority of the state as an undesirable restriction on the liberty of the individual. Thus in the nineteenth century one form of this is found in the urgings of the anarchists—Godwin, Proudhon, Kropotkin, etc.—who were prepared to condemn the concentration of political power, although they never went so far as to deny the legitimacy of power in any form.

Throughout these two millennia one could infer from the prevailing concepts of authority an underlying belief—a basically negative view of human nature which assumes that for the stability of society, humans need to be controlled by some sort of external authorities.

Authoritarian power throughout history has often yielded to the temptation to be repressive. Although the liberal theme has been strong in Western society for several centuries, anti-authoritarianism took a new spurt in reaction to the twentieth-century totalitarian state. An extreme form of this thrust is found in the neo-anarchists of the last third of the twentieth century, who insist on the natural, moral, social, intellectual, and personal equality of all individuals and hence challenge the legitimacy of *any* institution or relationship based on the pretended superiority of some individuals over others.

Examples abound of growing insistence on emancipation from external authority. Some, such as emancipation from the "expert," appear to be signs of wholesome growth. Others—juvenile truancy, vandalism, drug use and addictions, high rates of illegitimate births, increased crime rates, urban graffiti, and the anti-draft attitudes of the young—are more mixed, involving to some degree a rebellion against the authorized order but failure to replace it with suitable inner authority. Survey data in the U.S. and Western Europe shows a marked increase in distrust of authority, rising steadily since the late 1950s. Elsewhere in the world, stunning examples of the force of the emancipation movement are found in the recent peaceful uprisings in China and Eastern Europe.

The most fundamental challenge to authority, in some sense, is the contemporary questioning of the worldview put forth by scientific authorities. Starting in the late 1960s, the scientific priesthood has been progressively defrocked on two counts. The disastrous environmental and other effects of uninhibited applications of science and technology, the fears of nuclear weapons and new organisms from the enthusiasms of biotechnology have brought into question the automatic goodness of science. The "new transcendentalism" of growing numbers who have chosen to tap their "deep intuition" or "inner wisdom" have intensified questioning of the previously unquestioned truth of scientific knowledge.

The new locus of authority is within; a contemporary description is likely to speak of "taking back one's power" from external authorities. Of course this does not imply leading a lawless life. It does mean a kind of self-empowerment, psychological liberation, and a taking of responsibility for oneself. Aspects of this focus appear in varied places, including the self-help movements (especially as they deal with health, diet, nutrition, and personal development) and the psychological side of "decolonization" movements (such as development of pride in Native American or other native cultures; worker self-management; and feminist liberation from patriarchal institutions and mind-sets).

Being at peace and feeling empowered. Peace is all too frequently characterized as a bland, vaguely boring mode of existence characterized by the absence of strife or war. Contemporary peace and spiritual movements stress inner and interpersonal peace as the *norm*, rather than as the aberration.

Existential peace means much more than not fighting with neighbors, family, and co-workers. It implies the absence of any form of violence—such as addictions, masochistic activities, living in abusive situations which degrade and insult the self. It implies the presence of a sense of reverence for all of life, non-human as well as human, and an awareness of the unity of all creatures. With such a reverent attitude, living in peace is living gently on the Earth, and it is empowering, calling forth the growth of the individual, much as do the psychological, self-help and holistic health movements mentioned earlier.

The two modern movements of feminism and peace activism both imply this integration of inner peace and the empowerment of persons. Becoming empowered has been defined as the "process of discovering in one's self and others the capacity to make changes, affirming the authority we already have." (White and Van Soest, 1984; p. ii) Empowerment might be thought of as a form of awakening to the reality that we *are* powerful; that we *have* unique skills and talents that can serve the world around us, and bring betterment to the planet; that we *are* basically good and *can trust* ourselves and one another; that we *can* tap our courage, inner strength, creativity and spontaneity to make a difference in the world; that together we *can challenge* the legitimacy of any institution, no matter how powerful, because it is we the people who, in the end, give to that institution (or withhold) the perception of legitimacy.

Empowerment is the opposite of despair and passivity. It creates a feeling of excitement in life, and it leads to "chain reactions" that release the energy in others, which can serve to empower entire groups to do great things. As people work toward a shared goal, they come to discover their interconnectedness and self-value, in an environment of trust and service.

Respiritualization. The forces for change that have arisen during the last 30 years have been as much about a search for a new spirituality as they have been a search for a new social order. The values out of which the 1960s civil rights and anti-war movements grew were both spiritual—nonviolence and compassion—and democratic—freedom, equality, and self-determination. While some were acting out these values in social movements, others were seeking inner peace through a variety of spiritual disciplines and in an assortment of different traditions.

The search for inner peace brings about new ways of being and discovery of new dimensions of the self, which leads to reconceptualizing problems in much the same way as involvement in radical social change. For many there is a kind of *metanoia*, a conversion of the person's whole being. This may involve discovery of the spirit within, and a new awareness of the dignity of each life. While the spiritual and the political have often been viewed as separate aspects of life, increasingly they are perceived as two sides of the same coin.

The women's movement, in particular, combined the personal and the political through its emphasis on the immediate reality of individuals' lives. "The women's movement can be seen as a 'spiritual revolution'; it certainly bears witness to a new 'womanspirit rising.'... In our times 'spirituality' has become a more universal code word for the search for direction at a time of crisis." (King, 1989)

There is a growing tendency to blur any distinction between the secular and the spiritual. Both traditional and non-traditional forms of spiritual exploration, from creation spirituality to goddess religion, tend to include a social component. They encompass the spirituality which former Secretary General of the United Nations, U Thant, often spoke of as "the harmony between the innermost life and the outerlife, or the life of the world and the universe ... a serene comprehension of life in time and in space, the tuning of the inner person with the great mysteries and secrets around him ... a belief in the goodness of life, and the possibility of each human being to contribute his goodness to it." He "saw no difference between life and religion" and found "incomprehensible the Western distinction between secular and spiritual life." (Muller, 1982; pp. 41-46)

The respiritualization that is part of the contemporary cultural movement finds this separation between the spiritual and the material to be "altogether unwholesome.... Spirituality must not be understood as something added on to life. Rather, it is something which permeates all human activities and experiences rather than being additional to them." (King, 1989; p. 6) Indeed, it would appear to be crucial to the resolution of contemporary issues. As Morris Berman points out:

> The fundamental issues confronted by any civilization or by any person in his or her life are issues of meaning.... For more than 99 percent of human history, the world was enchanted, and man saw himself as an integral part of it. The complete reversal of this perception [in the modern Western world] has destroyed the continuity of the human experience and the integrity of the human psyche. It has very nearly wrecked the planet as well. The only hope ... lies in a reënchantment of the world. (Berman, 1981; p. 97)

The Overall Force for Change

The various trends and movements noted above support one another in such a way that it seems likely they will continue to grow in strength. Virtually no aspect of modern life or modern institutions will remain unaffected by these changes. Social relations; psychological images of human beings; economic conditions; political structures; technological inventions and their application or non-application; the conceptualization of problems; our faith in science; our attitudes about power, freedom, human potential—all these and more are currently in flux.

Not all the trends are new; some, in fact, are centuries old. What is new, however, is the way the strands are coming together (as Bishop Joseph Cardinal Bernardin has said) to weave a "seamless garment." It would be hard to find a time in history where there is such a confluence—of feminists, peace advocates, ecologists, economists, political theorists, social critics, futurists, psychologists, theologians, humanists, artists, writers, poets, inventors, scientists—all offering complementary pieces of the challenging puzzle that is "our common future."

What is the destination? Perhaps the overall change force can be reasonably well summed up in five components:

• *Search for wholeness.* By mid-century the world had become fragmented, as had the individual. With the rise of modern industrial capitalism the economy had become separate from, and dominant over, the rest of society. One's work in life had become a job, and the job was separate from the rest of life. The dominant mode of technocratic thinking, manipulative rationality, implied humanity's separation from the rest of nature, all of which became "resources" to be exploited in what ever ways would serve humankind. (Even other persons became "human resources" in the term prevalent throughout the corporate world.)

The attitude of man having dominion over nature and hence free to exploit the Earth in any way his whims move him was no doubt latent even in the wholeness of the medieval outlook. But the real rift between humankind and nature came from the seventeenth century onward, culminating in the all too familiar contemporary threats to not only ecological systems and endangered species, but even the Earth's basic life-support systems.

In a variety of ways—implicit in the women's movement, the ecological movement, the holistic health movement, the emphasis on quality of work life, the appropriate technology movement, the human rights and peace movements—the perception was being expressed that life is whole, and there is something fundamentally wrong with a society that breaks it into fragments.

• *Search for community.* Both urbanization and modern economic realities—most jobs away from home and neighborhood—have brought about a sense of loss of community. The response has many forms: intentional communities; re-ruralization and decentralization movements; crafts movements; informal economies; and an assortment of human relations workshops, group therapies, and other endeavors to relate more deeply with fellow human beings.

• *Search for identity.* Resistance has grown toward the homogenization to which modern society is prone, with its mass markets and mass media. Some of those most overtly expressing this are ethnic groups—Palestinian, Québecois, Basque, Chicano. Others are different in other ways, but asserting their right to be themselves and not feel or be treated as inferior—the handicapped, the aged. The two largest such groups are women and ex-colonials. Both are struggling to release themselves from their self-perception as inferior, a consequence of generations of domination by the white-male mindset. Both of these represent *majority* population groups. Their awakening could by itself change the world.

• *Search for meaning.* Michael Maccoby (1988) finds the drive for meaning to be the strongest of all our value drives, the one which ultimately shapes all the rest. Western society in the latter third of the century is clearly suffering a crisis of meaning and values. With the "great debunking" of religion by reductionist, positivistic science, and the subsequent discovery that economic production is inadequate as the focal meaning of a society, there has developed a total absence of consensus in the area of basic values and central meaning. As a response to this vacuum there are many signs of a renewed search for spiritual values, including a reassessment of the kind of science that had driven them out a half century earlier. This search admittedly takes on some dogmatic, fundamentalist forms at one end of the spectrum and some rather "flaky" forms at the other end. Probably its most important aspects are 1) the shift from seeking the "right" external authority to a focus on discovering the source of inner wisdom; and 2) the quiet infusion of the "new meaning" into all forms of business and professional life.

• *Search for personal power.* Many signs over the past quarter century point to people's rising sense of their own power to change their lives, and the world. People are awakening to the fact that whether the issue is polluting technology or nuclear terror, they have the power to challenge the legitimacy of the existing order. In the feminist movement, the deep ecology movement, the search for a science going "beyond reductionism," and in some of the nativist movements in the developing world, one senses that *what is really at issue is the basic legitimacy of the tendency for the Western industrial paradigm to dominate the world.*

Within these five components of the change force, two themes stand out: 1) an emphasis on wholeness, unity, interconnectedness; and 2) an emphasis on inner authority, integrity, discovering inner knowing and wisdom, drawing on hidden inner resources. These characteristics comprise a powerful force for, and invitation to, societal transformation, opposing contemporary tendencies toward fragmentation, alienation, materialism, and manipulative rationality.

Part of the wide appeal of this powerful and meaningful invitation to transformation is that no one is left out. It is not a revolution carried out by armies, nor a "knowledge revolution" in the hands of experts.

Every individual is called to self-transformation, and to playing a role in the transformation of society. Because every aspect of the society is involved in the transformation, identifying a suitable role is no problem. Wherever one is is a good place to start.

Chapter 4

Features of the
Emerging Society

A transfiguration from modern to trans-modern society is plausible because of the convergence of *two powerful and growing social forces:* one, the growing awareness that the present order does not well serve people, communities, future generations, nor the planet in the long run; the other, the spreading vision of a just, harmonious, and sustainable world within our grasp.

From the dilemmas facing contemporary society, which we explored in Chapter 2, we can get some idea of the features that will have to change if human society is to survive and prosper. From the goals sought in the various social movements surveyed in Chapter 3, we get clues as to the probable form of the society to which all this is leading. Let us explore some salient characteristics of the society that seems to be aborning by considering these two forces together.

Public awareness of the predicament of modern society is especially focused on the natural environment. One can hardly fail to be aware of the numerous environmental disasters of recent years. The fact that economic activities are having an effect on the climate, and will have more, seems firmly established. The problems of air and water pollution, environmental degradation, extinction of species, desertification, deforestation, soil erosion, toxic chemical concentrations, ozone depletion—these are so well known that we are somewhat numbed from hearing about them. It is ever more apparent that the solution of such problems involves much more than patching up with corrective legislation and other ameliorative measures. One has to be concerned with the drive for increasing economic growth and the correlation between that growth and the environmental costs; with the kinds of technologies used and the kinds of products produced; with the continual urging via the advertising industry to consume more prodigally and improvidently. Behind all of these are the driving values of the economy.

It is a hard lesson to learn, that there is nothing in the way of specific actions by government or business that can do more than slow the rate at which these problems are avalanching down upon us. *There is no solution, short of reinventing modern society.* So we shall look first at the deep-level shift in value patterns which Riane Eisler has characterized as a shift from "dominator" patriarchal society to a "partnership society."

Even more fundamental than values is the perception of reality from which the values emerge. Since the picture of reality held in modern society is so strongly influenced by what science tells us is real, it is necessary to examine the indications of a change in the fundamental bias of Western science. Here it is easier to describe what we are moving away from that hasn't worked than to discern what we are moving toward. However, it seems safe to predict that a new spirituality is on the rise—a spirituality less institutionalized and sacerdotal than in the past, but more subtly permeating the whole of society.

Finally, we will bring all of this to bear in attempting to discern the future form of the economy and the structuring of work to serve both the individual and society.

Reassessing Technology and Patriarchal Society

There can be little doubt that society's use of technology and its future are closely intertwined. Technology is hero or villain, depending on how you look at it. Humankind has reached the point where one can hardly imagine any technological goal that could not be accomplished, if the necessary resources and time were devoted. The question is: What is worth doing? And there modern society has been extraordinarily confused.

A measure of our confusion is that we continue to try to solve the problems that have been brought about or exacerbated by our use of technology—with more technology used in the same way! The most egregious example is Star Wars to combat the threat of nuclear missiles, but there are others: attempting to cure ecological insults brought about by our use of technology through a "pollution control industry"; dealing with illness caused in part by modern lifestyles through interventions such as chemotherapy and radiation that further impair the natural healing and defense systems; seeking technological cures for chronic poverty and hunger that are themselves the consequences of industrial society impinging on other cultures.

The emergence of post-patriarchal society. Riane Eisler, in her analysis of the ills of patriarchal society, has proposed a somewhat broader than usual definition of technology: *Technology is a dynamic process of using tools, resources, bodies, and minds to achieve human-defined goals.* Focusing on ends rather than means, she defines four basic categories of technology:

1. *Technologies of production.* This includes farming, weaving, manufacturing, construction, and other ways in which tasks are carried out to sustain and enhance human life.
2. *Technologies of reproduction and regeneration.* This includes birthing procedures, birth control techniques, replacement of bodily parts (with prosthetics, artificial organs, organ transplants, etc.), in vitro fertilization, etc.
3. *Technologies of actualization.* These include social technologies such as public education, democratic political processes, art forms, actualization workshops, etc., as well as personal technologies like meditation for spiritual growth, biofeedback training for self-healing, and so on.
4. *Technologies of destruction.* These are technologies aimed at destroying and dominating. They range from the primitive techniques of individual combat to vast systems for delivering nuclear warheads and biological and chemical weapons.

Classifying in this way makes clear a critical choice of the future—that of life-destroying versus life-enhancing technologies. By and large, of course, people don't feel that they are making life-destroying choices. (We may feel that someone else is, and thus feel forced into a life-destroying technology policy like nuclear deterrence.) But we are part of a vast social matrix that in the end generates the choices. Thus the question becomes relevant: What kind of social organization would give priority to technologies of production, reproduction, and actualization, and minimize the use of technologies of destruction?

Eisler's reading of the historical and archeological evidence suggests that Neolithic societies may indeed have had these priorities. Their social organization seems to have been basically egalitarian; differences in status and wealth were not marked. Women were not subordinate to men: There were women priestesses and women craftspeople, and the supreme deity was characterized as female rather than male. The primary principle of social organization seems to have been *linking* by mutual trust and caring, rather than ranking and dominating based on force. These attributes seem also to be characteristic of many of the societies of indigenous peoples that still remain on all five continents. Unfortunately, most of us in modern society were educated to believe that we have nothing to learn from these "primitive" cultures.

Eisler introduces the term "partnership society," in contrast to "dominator society," for the social organization in which male-female difference is *not* equated with superiority-inferiority; "feminine values" such as caring, compassion, empathy, sensitivity, and gentleness can operationally be given social priority; and life-enhancing technologies can have precedence. Just how closely this ideal was approached by ancient societies is a matter for scholars to haggle over, but its merit as a pattern for the future is obvious.

This line of reasoning suggests that the contemporary feminist movement should not be viewed as essentially another movement for civil rights, equal opportunities, and equal pay for equal work—nor even primarily as a movement for raising "feminine consciousness." The reassertion of the importance of the feminine is in a sense more fundamental than any of the social movements, underlying the peace and ecological movements, hunger projects, and civil rights movements. It is a basic movement away from the hierarchical, aggressive, exploitative, dominator kind of organization which is associated with all of our most serious problems, and a movement toward a caring, partnership organization that can give us a chance to have a more viable global future.

If it is true that we must shift from a dominator to a partnership model of social organization, this change, by definition, cannot be brought about by violence. This cannot be the classical revolution of history books, for technologies of destruction can only replace one dominator system with another. This revolution must be, fundamentally, a transformation of human consciousness. It must involve a reassessment of the basic "picture of reality" which underlies our science, our technology, and our systems of education and communication. That is why we turn now to the need for a restructuring of Western science.

The Reconstruction of Science

It has been becoming clear for some time that modern science is in crisis. One might think that even if this is true, it is a matter for the scientists to straighten out. But because of the profound implications of this crisis for values and meanings, for those navigational signals by which we attempt to guide our lives and society, the matter is too important to leave to the scientists. It is, in the most basic sense, a political issue of concern to every member of society.

It is a crisis of *causality*; one involving scientific explanations about what *causes* things. The concepts of scientific explanation which have reigned for many generations are being questioned in a way that is more fundamental than any such questioning since the revolutionary shift, in the seventeenth century, associated with names like Galileo and Newton. Because this questioning affects every aspect of modern society, we must give the issue special attention.

Now you could interview a long list of scientists and have a fairly high probability that not one of them would speak of a crisis in causality. Yet philosophers of science have been aware of it some time. The realization that science had to strain so to exclude volition, or will, was a chief ground for suspicion regarding its adequacy as a final descriptor of reality. In fact, it was clear to any competent philosopher that the conventional scientific concept of causation could not give a *complete* explanation of anything, even in principle.

Let us put this in the simplest possible terms. If in this interactive system we call the universe, everything is really connected to everything, then a change anywhere in the system will affect every element of the system, no matter how minutely. In other words, *everything is the cause of everything else.* However true that statement may be, the way of looking at phenomena which it suggests is too complex to be of any practical use. But there are two special ways of looking that are extremely useful. One is that of *scientific causality*, where a tiny bit of the universe is considered to be sufficiently in isolation that a reductionistic explanation (for example, gas temperature in terms of the motions of the molecules; human behavior in terms of stimulus and response) leads to adequate predictability. The other is that of *volitional causality.* We employ this in our everyday dealings with persons. It is useful for situations where the effects of human conscious and unconscious choice are large compared with other effects. It is this kind of cause that is of interest in the courtroom when seeking the motivation for a crime.

In short, scientific causality is *never* more than an approximation, useful for certain purposes. The concepts and interactions with which science deals are an abstraction from the greater reality; they model parts of reality in ways that are helpful when one is interested in being able to control or manipulate the physical environment. When science proved to be extremely efficacious in that regard, and seemingly effective in explaining such matters as the evolution of stars, planets, and life forms, its prestige and influence grew. To much of the public, and to many of the scientists, the models of science became mistaken for reality itself. The fact that this science essentially denied the presence of volitional causality, in spite of the latter's obviously important role, was somehow overlooked. And so a lot of fruitless debates persisted, such as the famous one about "free will versus determinism."

In our everyday practical living we don't have much confusion about the fact that these quite different kinds of "causes" are true at the same time. You need them both to get a complete understanding. But in the world of science it is different. The volitional cause tends to involve *teleological factors* (issues of design or purpose) and *conscious choice*, and these are in essence *ruled out of consideration*. Science can't deal with these, and many, perhaps most, scientists insist that volitional causes don't really exist—that what appears to be "free will" can in principle be explained in terms of "more fundamental" causes, such as genetic inheritance, conditioned habit patterns, and so on.

Consciousness as causal. The puzzle of conscious awareness is perhaps the most fundamental of all, particularly at the level of the human organism. Arthur Koestler (*The Invisible Writing*) offers a personal reflection on this puzzle in his description of experiences of deprivation during long days of imprisonment in the Spanish Civil War:

> [These experiences] had filled me with a direct certainty that a higher order of reality existed, and that it alone invested experience with meaning. I came to call it later on 'the reality of the third order.' The narrow world of sensory perception constituted the first order; this perceptual world was enveloped by the conceptual world which contained phenomena not directly perceivable, such as gravitation, electromagnetic fields, and curved space. The second order of reality filled in the gaps and gave meaning to the absurd patchiness of the sensory world. In the same manner, the third order of reality enveloped, interpenetrated, and gave meaning to the second. It contained

'occult' phenomena which could not be apprehended or explained either on the sensory or the conceptual level, and yet occasionally invaded them like spiritual meteors piercing the primitive's vaulted sky. Just as the conceptual order showed up the illusions and distortions of the senses, so the 'third order' disclosed that time, space and causality, that isolation, separateness, and spatio-temporal limitations of the self were merely optical illusions on the next higher level.

Whereas the esoteric "perennial wisdom" of the world's spiritual traditions deals centrally with Koestler's "third order of reality," modern science is mainly antagonistic and skeptical. In the positivistic faith of mainstream science, mind or consciousness is epiphenomenal; that is, it is derivative from the physical and chemical processes going on in the brain and need not be separately understood. There is no room in this science for such a totally heretical statement as a recent observation of Nobel laureate biologist George Wald. Wald has concerned himself in his later years with the question of why the universe seems so favorable to the development of life. He wrote recently that he believes the conventional concept, of consciousness appearing only very late in the evolutionary process, is wrong; rather, it appears that *consciousness was present all along:*

> A few years ago it occurred to me ... that mind, rather than being a very late development in the evolution of living things, restricted to organisms with the most complex nervous systems— all of which I had believed to be true—that mind instead has been there always, and that this universe is life-breeding because the pervasive presence of mind had guided it to be so. That thought ... so offended my scientific possibilities as to embarrass me. It took only a few weeks, however, to realize that I was in excellent company. That line of thought is not only deeply embedded in millennia-old Eastern philosophies—but it has been expressed plainly by a number of great and very recent physicists [Eddington, Schrödinger, Pauli among others]. (Wald, 1988)

In our everyday life experience, consciousness is primary; it is through conscious awareness that we understand anything at all, and that we carry out our most cherished actions. Nobel laureate neuroscientist Roger Sperry has been most forceful in insisting that science can never be fully adequate until it recognizes "inner conscious awareness as a causal reality." (Sperry, 1981)

In a recent (1987) paper, Sperry urges inclusion into science of what he terms "downward causation," (volitional causation) according to which "things are controlled not only from below upward by atomic and molecular action but also from above downward by mental, social, political, and other macro properties. [Furthermore,] primacy is given to the higher level controls rather than the lowest."

But to reap the full benefits of the scientific mode of inquiry it will be necessary to give scientific validity to complementary explanations as well—that is, to explaining the lower level in terms of the higher.

Problems with the present paradigm of Western science. If this confusion about causality presents a problem in science, however, it is in its impacts on society that it wreaks even more mischief. Because science has been so remarkably successful in the creation of technology, its worldview has gained tremendous prestige. The scientific picture of reality tends to be accepted throughout society as pretty much the final word. But if that accepted picture of the one "reality" systematically omits some of the causality pattern, then society's actions are being based on an erroneous perception of the world.

For example, society surely is confused about its educational institutions: What are the goals of education? Educational practitioners are strongly influenced by the prevailing interpretation of scientific causality; from this it seems reasonable to think of education as primarily conditioning, "socialization," teaching knowledge and skills. However with a different interpretation, involving conscious and unconscious choices, the tasks of self-understanding and freeing inner creativity would receive far more emphasis.

In our legal institutions, to take another example, people are assumed to be responsible for their acts—acts which may result in a person being executed or incarcerated for life. If at the same time society's scientific institutions are claiming that those acts have their root cause in the person's DNA and childhood conditioning (in which case the person would be blameless no matter what he did), then surely we are confused about justice.

Society's accepted framework of values, ethics and meanings is ultimately based in some cosmology; some "picture" of the nature of the universe and our relationship to it; some "story" about how we came to be here. In the case of nineteenth-century European and American culture, this was the centuries-old Christian "story" of a transcendent deity who became incarnate to save humans from the consequences of their original sin, together with a scientific "story" that relegated the Creator to someplace outside the universe, and gave "Him" the role of "clockmaker." Small wonder, then, that many people were disturbed when the old causality framework was challenged by the Darwinian story of the causes of evolution, and the Freudian story of the causes of human development. They sensed, decades before it happened, that this spelled the end of any consensus about meanings and values. By mid-twentieth century modern man (especially, but woman too!) was extremely confused about values.

The nature of our present societal and global problems reflects that confusion. Our sense of who we are and what kind of universe we are in has a profound effect on how we let economic activity exploit the natural environment. It affects how we perceive our relationships to the other creatures of the Earth, and hence our treatment of them. It influences our view of death and hence the national health care bill with its exorbitantly expensive, "heroic" measures taken to extend the life span of the dying. The more one thinks about it, the more clear becomes the relationship between our explanations of "why things happen" and the kinds of ecological, political, and social problems we create for ourselves.

Throughout all of this there is an evident paradox. If, as so many so confidently claimed, modern science was closing in on an ever more adequate description of reality, replacing the kinds of explanations found in traditional cultures with more "scientific" explanations, how does it happen that so many in contemporary society are now finding wisdom in the insights of traditional cultures and spiritual disciplines? Those who are so inclined are often among the most well educated, and not simply seeking emotional comfort or escape.

Thus, even as modern science was achieving its greatest triumphs in terms of new technologies in such areas as satellites, computers, artificial intelligence, and biotechnology, there were many—scientists as well as nonscientists—who suspected that something was fundamentally wrong with the scientific picture. To understand the origin of the crisis in science in slightly more detail, one has to go back to its formative period.

Science's underlying metaphysical assumptions. Ever since the discovery of unconscious processes and the extent to which our perceptions are shaped by unconsciously held beliefs, it has been apparent that Western science (like the belief system of any other society) *could* be fundamentally mistaken. Western science is an artifact of Western society. Its shaping aims for three centuries and more have been prediction and control and consequent ability to manipulate the physical environment. As a consequence, it does very well at prediction and control in certain limited ways.

By the early eighteenth century the upstart science had adopted a base of metaphysical assumptions upon which the structure of later scientific developments was to rest. One of these was the *objectivist* assumption, that the observer could separate himself from that being observed, and learn about it through various kinds of probes—electron beams, electromagnetic waves, etc. A second was the *positivist* assumption, that what is scientifically real is what is measurable. A third was the *reductionist* assumption, that the cause of a complex phenomenon can be completely understood in terms of more elemental events, for example, explanation of the operation of a computer chip in terms of the movement of electrons in the silicon base. These, it is important to recognize, are not three scientific *findings*, but rather, a priori *assumptions*.

These assumptions limited the scope of inquiry of the new science to the aspects of reality that are physically measurable, and to explanations that are nonteleological and fragmented. This initial limiting was a perfectly reasonable thing to do, and prudently avoided theological conflicts. However, as science gained more and more power and prestige, there was a tendency to gloss over the fact that the entire scientific edifice was built upon some rather arbitrary metaphysical assumptions and to assume that the partial reality described by this science is instead the whole.

This inadvertent error had a pervasive effect. A major aim of the scientific enterprise had been to substitute scientific explanations for prescientific superstitions; thus there was considerable concern that the doors not be opened to the sorts of miraculous happenings so easily accepted by the prescientific mind. Scientists felt a necessity to deny the validity of a host of phenomena and types of experience that didn't fit within the limits set by the three assumptions listed above. Throughout the history of modern science, a tremendous amount of effort has gone into defending the barricades against, or explaining away, not only these outcasts, including miraculous healings and psychic phenomena, but also more ordinary experiences such as volition, intention, conscious awareness, selective attention, and the multifold ways in which people experience the noumenal or spiritual.

In other words, Western science early took a form that automatically excluded those characteristics typically found in a traditional, spiritual, or metaphysical worldview. It was impossible within that science to understand such beliefs, and the experiences on which they were based, in terms that did not distort their meaning. Rather, these "animistic religions" and "prescientific superstitions" tended to be explained away in terms of a desire to control one's environment through magic, or to recreate the feelings of safety in the mother's womb.

The revaluing of traditional belief systems that has been taking place over the past couple of decades poses a puzzling question. If these traditional, often shamanistic, belief systems reflect valid aspects of human experience, how can science be reconciled with that validity? How can science be restructured, waiving the three metaphysical assumptions on which it has been based, and assuming instead that *any class of inner experiences that have been reported, or of phenomena that have been observed, down through the ages and across cultures, apparently in some sense exist and have a face validity that cannot be denied?*

Such a restructuring of science may not be as difficult a task as it might seem at first thought. (Harman, 1988) Neither is it as discontinuous as it might sound. As one would expect, it would leave most of present science intact, complementing rather than contradicting that tested knowledge. The two main changes would appear to be: 1) research methods will need to include more participative modes of inquiry; and 2) both reductionistic and volitional causality will need to be admitted as forms of explanation. The most significant impact of the restructuring on society would be the reconciling of the disunitive "two cultures" of modern society which C.P. Snow wrote about three decades ago—the one culture of science, technology, and the economy, and the other culture of the humanities and religion. (Snow, 1959)

Deeper significance of the restructuring. One of the implications of this sort of extended science is at the same time one of the reasons it has been long in coming about. In participatory research, especially into areas involving human consciousness, the very experience of observing brings about sensitization and other changes in the observer. Thus, *a willingness to be transformed is an essential characteristic of the participatory scientist.* The anthropologist who would see clearly another culture than her own must allow that experience to change her so that the new culture is seen through new eyes, not eyes conditioned by the scientist's own culture. In order to see his client clearly, the psychotherapist must have worked through his own neuroses which would otherwise warp perception. So the scientist who would explore the spiritual wisdom within the traditional cultures must be willing to go through the deep changes that will make him or her a competent observer. Each of us has some resistance to such change.

In the past, scientists have tended to insist that teleological and value-focused questions are not appropriate to science. Of course, some such questions have always been asked, for example in the area of health sciences: A question about the function of some part of the body's regulatory system is teleological, and certainly a question about what leads toward health is value-focused.

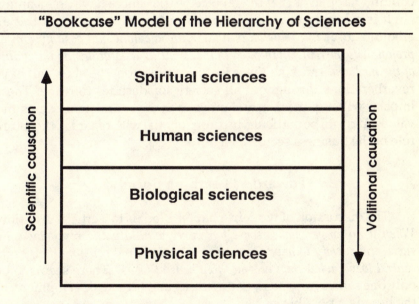

"Bookcase" Model of the Hierarchy of Sciences

Now we see that this prejudice of science is really a matter of levels in the hierarchy of understanding. Teleological questions have no place at the level of reductionistic science of physical reality. At the level of biological sciences, however, it is appropriate to ask about the function of elaborate instinctive patterns in animal behavior. At the level of the human sciences, volition is acceptable as a causal factor, and personality characteristics are meaningful constructs. In exploring the deepest insights of traditional cultures and our heritage of the world's religions, one may encounter the concept of "other realities" experienced through non-ordinary states of consciousness.

The restructuring of science is directly relevant to the plight of modern society. The analysis of Chapter 3 showed that some kind of "respiritualizing" impulse is inherent in contemporary social movements, viewed as a whole. However, enriching modern society through the insights of the spiritual pioneers in the traditional cultures and world religious traditions goes hand in hand with restructuring Western science which has constituted such a barrier. The latter is required to reconcile the human experience of spirituality with the material-world picture that comes out of the investigations of mainstream science. The realm of the spiritual has played a significant role in all cultures, and in history. Science in the past has been rather unaccepting of these matters, insisting that the reported phenomena couldn't happen or that the reported experiences have no meaning.

It is sobering to realize what a fundamental-level shift this all amounts to: *It is a revision of underlying metaphysical assumptions as profound as the revision implicit in the scientific revolution and the ending of the medieval era.* Like the scientific revolution, the shift will have reverberations throughout all society for decades to come. These impacts will be particularly significant in the realm of meanings and values, and will be particularly consequential with regard to the future role of the business sector.

Toward a "Learning Society"

The discussion of work in Chapter 1 led us to a crucial question: *When it no longer makes sense for an economically and technologically successful society to have economic production (and consumption) as its central focus, what then becomes that central focus?* There seems to be only one satisfactory answer—learning and human development, in the broadest possible sense.

The term "The Learning Society" was defined in 1968 by Robert Hutchins in a book by that title. It is a society in which the primary goals of the society comprise—for the individual—learning, fulfillment, and fully actualizing one's unique potentialities; and— for the group—ennobling social enterprises. The "learning society" has such goals and "all its institutions [are] directed to this end. This is what the Athenians did.... They made their society one designed to bring all the members to the fullest development of their highest powers.... Education was not a segregated activity, conducted for certain hours, in certain places, at a certain time of life. It was the aim of the society.... The Athenian was educated by his culture, by *Paideia*." (To be sure, the Greeks had slaves rather than high technology, so the two societies are not strictly comparable. Nevertheless, the principle of lifelong learning taking place in all society's institutions is fully applicable.)

Paideia was the educating matrix of the society, shaping all its institutions. "*Paideia* is education looked upon as a lifelong transformation of the human personality, in which every aspect of life plays a part.... [It is] the task of giving form to the act of living itself: treating every occasion of life as a means of self-fabrication.... *Paideia* is not merely a learning: it is a making and a shaping; and man himself is the work of art that *paideia* seeks to form.... The lesson of *paideia* is fundamentally the prime lesson of democracy: Growth and self-transformation cannot be delegated." (Mumford, 1956) The highest and central theme of *paideia* was the inner journey, "the search for the Divine Center."

The basic concept underlying the "learning society" is that learning in the broadest sense—education, research, exploration, developing self-understanding, and participating in the community of concerned citizens to choose a better future—contributes to human betterment and fulfillment. These activities are humane, nonpolluting, and nonstultifying; they can absorb unlimited numbers of persons not required for other sorts of work. In a society centered around the goal of learning there would be no "superfluous people." *Learning is both end and means.*

The "learning society" can not be designed and managed from the top down. However, that does not make its emergence less plausible; after all, the same could be said for our present society. No one set out to design the modern industrial economy. As the underlying belief system emerged out of its medieval predecessor, and the associated new patterns of motivation arose, people and groups of people solved the problems they perceived in their own local ways. Modern society gradually took on its present form through an ecological, organic sort of transformation. Some experiments succeeded and were copied; other experiments failed or died off. Some broad organizing patterns developed, of course—for example, the Constitution of the United States, the Charter of the United Nations. But those largely ordered what already existed; they were important but minor modifications to a system already in being.

Some of the basic features of that system turn out not to work very well for the future. One of these is the idea that, progressively, practically everything in human life becomes monetized and part of one huge economy. The disadvantages of this have become so apparent that all sorts of experiments with new communities, local informal economies, etc. are being tried, and some of them seem to work rather well. Another aspect of the present system that works less and less well, as we have seen, is the equating of work with jobs in the mainstream economy. *Once the mind is freed by separating the functions of creative work and income distribution, unbounded opportunities become apparent.*

Everyone in the "learning society" can be involved in learning and creative work; it does not depend on generating jobs through economic growth. The motivation for learning and creative work is intrinsic in people; it is but necessary to remove the blocks. The idea that people are motivated only by desire for economic gain is part of the Western industrial paradigm; it appears true only because we have been conditioned to believe it. (Consider how the great Gothic cathedrals were built; we find it hard today to imagine the religious fervor motivating the skilled craftsmen who performed these remarkable feats.)

The social-roles function of work is enhanced when work is mainly done in the environment of the home, community, or small corporation. The best source of sufficient and satisfactory work roles is in the multitudinous activities involved in a learning and consciously evolving society. Many such roles are in the "third," or "voluntary" sector—which emphasizes the observation that part of our problem here is in the tight coupling between work and income. No society need ever run out of constructive work roles—that situation only occurs when all such roles are assumed to have to come from the activity of economic production and to be located in the monetized mainstream economy.

As to distribution of wealth and income, there are any number of ways this might be done. Taking the small community as a basic unit, distribution could be partly on the basis of membership and partly on the basis of a local economy. Malingerers are no more a serious problem than they are in a large family.

Thus the "learning society" we imagine is quite decentralized. Its technology tends to be environmentally benign, resource conserving, frugal in its use of energy, and understandable and usable at the individual or community level—"appropriate" or "intermediate." (E.F. Schumacher) It tends to complement a strong ecological ethic; identification with nature, fellow human beings, and future generations; a lifestyle characterized by voluntary frugality ("doing more with less"); appreciation of the simple life and simple virtues; and the work that fosters these attitudes.

Possible New Economic Structures

The present structure of the economy, including its underlying values, is fraught with paradoxes and contradictions. The economy rests on the ecology—on the life-support systems of the planet, the mineral and fossil fuel resources that have been stored up over eons, the resources and waste-absorbing capacity of the natural environment. Yet the inherent incentive system in the economy works against preserving the natural environment, against frugal use of the stored resources, against minimizing the unpredictable impact of economic activities on the climate, against conserving the spirit-renewing wilderness.

The economy presumably exists to serve people; yet in many ways people end up serving the economy. Economic values and rationality tend to push out more humane considerations. As E.F. Schumacher insisted,

> The science of economics does not stand on its own feet; it is derived from a view of the meaning and purpose of life—whether the economist himself knows this or not. And ... the only fully developed system of economic thought that exists at present is derived from a purely materialistic view of life.

The unnoticed economy. Hazel Henderson (1988) emphasizes economists' tendency to describe only part of the productive system of an industrial society. The total system includes the following "layers":

- *Private Sector*—production, employment, consumption, investment, savings as monetized and officially measured in the economic statistics.
- *Public Sector*—national, state, and local government; infrastructure (roads, maintenance, sewers, bridges, subways, schools, municipal services, etc.) (also counted in the official economic statistics).
- *"Underground Economy"*—illegal, tax-dodging cash-based exchanges (estimated to be as large as 15 percent of the

measured economic exchange in the U.S. and more in some countries).

- *Social Cooperative "Counter-Economy"*—"sweat-equity," do-it-yourself, bartering; home-based production for own use; subsistence agriculture; social, familial, and community structures; unpaid housework and parenting, volunteering, sharing; mutual aid, caring for the old and sick (non-monetized altruism and sharing—subsidizes the official economy with unpaid labor).
- *Nature*—natural resource base, waste absorption and recycling (subsidizes the official economy by unaccounted or absorbed environmental costs).

If the activities in the "counter-economy" and the value of the services performed by nature were counted, they are estimated to be comparable with the entire official public and private sector economies. The value of exchanges and services in the household economy alone has been estimated to be more than all the wages and salaries paid out by all of the corporations in the U.S., and the capitalization (in homes, automobiles, home appliances, etc.) to be more than all of the capital value of those corporations. The socially indispensable work of the informal (or "counter") economy has always provided the cooperative social framework within which the highly regarded competition of the marketplace could achieve its "successes." Clearly the official statistics present a very warped picture of the production system.

This becomes an important consideration as we go through a transition (as we must) from economies that maximize production and are based on nonrenewable resources to economies that minimize waste, recycle everything possible, depend as much as possible on renewable resources, and are managed for sustained-yield productivity (the way that farming used to be done).

But all of that could be done and we would still not have solved our most pressing problems if the economy is still driven by the need for growth to create jobs and high returns on capital investment. One of the social movements discussed in Chapter 2 is toward a decentralized economy, local informal economies, and self-created work opportunities. This probably points to one of the salient characteristics of trans-industrial society, one feature of which is the home.

The home has been considered by economists as the basic *consumption* unit. As emphasized by Alvin Toffler (1981) and Hazel

Henderson (1988), we are beginning to see the home emerging as a *production* unit, as it was before the Industrial Revolution. (This trend is subtly resisted by the system. We have some "cottage industry" legislation on the books that serves to oppose the trend. Corporations are allowed to deduct, for tax purposes, their capital costs and depreciation; however, householders are forced to treat their productive assets as consumables.) Part of this is things like home repair, "do-it-yourself" furniture manufacture, local energy supply (solar collectors, windmills), home canning, etc. Partly it is small businesses run out of the home.

Another important feature is the emergence of multitudinous local economies. Chapter 2 noted the deleterious effects of combined debtor society mentality and tolerance of high interest rates. It is almost impossible to imagine a way in which that situation could be easily reversed. On the other hand, we already have many examples of spontaneous emergence of local economies; enough of them would effectively destructure the mainstream economy. Furthermore, the local economies give a resilience to the local community and help it to weather a stormy transition period such as may be coming.

A working local economy. A typical example is the "Local Employment Trading System" (LETS) initiated by Michael Linton in Courtenay, British Columbia. In essence, this is a local economy with its own currency called "green dollars," which is not printed money but electronic signals on a computer system. You might say it is a computer-aided barter system. Say I need to have my house painted. I agree with the painter to pay X amount of "green dollars" and Y amount of Canadian dollars. (He needs the Canadian dollars to buy paint, which is not manufactured in the community.) With his "green dollars" the painter can buy services or manufactured items from others within the community. If I need to borrow "green dollars" from the system, the loan is interest-free; because of that feature, the local currency circulates much more rapidly than the Canadian money. Thus it comes about that the community has a flourishing economy even when the surrounding provincial economy is in a depressed state.

Hope on the development front. The Foundation for International Community Assistance (FINCA) of Tucson, Arizona, affords another example of how ordinary citizens are sensing the need and responding to it. John Hatch is an entrepreneur who made an important observation about the development puzzle. It is simply this: The poor already have the ingenuity, the knowledge, and the motivation to help themselves; often the main thing they need is capital. Throughout the developing world, in the villages, are hundreds of thousands of persons with the talent to start a small business if only a credit line of, say, $100, were available; however, that is precisely what they cannot get from governments, banks, or development agencies. It is commonly known that most of the assistance to developing countries from organizations like AID and major foundations ends up benefiting established businessmen and wealthier farmers. Most help for severely poor families has been granted in the form of food subsidies, which offer only temporary alleviation and leave them trapped in a vicious cycle of poverty. Hatch's response to this was FINCA.

FINCA makes funds available to communities to establish revolving loan funds, or "village banks." Self-managing local members decide on which community-wide income-generating projects are undertaken and which small individual loans are made. No collateral other than the individual's honor and signature (or thumbprint) is required. Example businesses include buying and selling fruits or vegetables, tortilla manufacture, sewing clothes, raising small livestock, crafting ceramics, and weaving. Loan repayments are made on a weekly basis and include a savings component which entitles borrowers to qualify for an ever-increasing credit line. Failure to repay is rare. Hatch found that the poorest of the poor can make astonishingly good use of even the smallest amount of credit without expensive training or technology. He believes that the entrepreneurial potential of women constitutes one of the least-utilized resources in development; the great majority of FINCA loans are to women.

The FINCA example is of interest both to exemplify the potentiality of local-initiative approaches to recalcitrant problems, and to show how an individual entrepreneur with a fresh idea can make a significant difference. When the interconnected problems described in Chapter 2 find their ultimate resolution, it will no doubt incorporate these two factors.

Intimations of a New Society

Awareness of the threats from economic activity to natural ecological communities and the Earth's life-support systems, and the threat of uncontrollable human-made climate change, has been growing rapidly. In the society envisioned by the "Green" movements the consume-and-waste ethic of industrial society is replaced by an *ecological ethic* and a *self-realization ethic*.

The ecological ethic involves identification with the whole of nature, from the smallest life form to the planet itself and the evolutionary forces that prevail there. It calls for humankind to act in partnership with nature in protecting the complex life-support systems of the planet; to husband resources appropriately; to modify ecological relationships wisely; to re-establish satisfactory recycling relationships in harmony with natural ones; and to move toward a new economic-ecological system that makes a clear distinction between wholesome and cancerous forms of growth.

The self-realization ethic affirms that the proper end of all individual experience is the furthering of individual awareness and the evolutionary development of the human species in harmony with Earth and all its creatures. The appropriate function of all social institutions is to create environments that will foster this awareness and development.

These new ethics require a transformation of the economic system. James Robertson (1979) identifies 11 features of the new "equilibrium" economy:

1. Ecologically sound, frugal, depending largely on renewable energy sources;
2. Lower throughput, greater durability of products;
3. People first, things second;
4. Greater local, regional national self-sufficiency;
5. A more decentralized economy;
6. International economic activity "harnessed to the common objective of helping each region and country become more self-sufficient";
7. Appropriate technology—"good to work with, sparing in its use of resources, producing a good end-product, and kind to the environment";
8. Revitalized town and country; de-urbanization;
9. Greater economic equality;

10. Merging of work, leisure, and life;
11. "Decolonization" of the institutionalized economy; reversal of the trend for more and more to shift from informal to formal economy.

The necessary change in our concept of science was discussed above. Signs of this change are less visible than the signs of economic rethinking, but its seeds are present in the spread of a new metaphysic in the culture at large.

Thus a scenario becomes increasingly plausible in which the industrialized world shifts, in Eisler's terms, from a dominator to a partnership society, and the values which are labeled feminine are fully integrated into the guidance mechanisms of society. It includes emergence of a more politically and economically balanced system. One of the most dramatic consequences of this shift is the possibility that throughout the world we will live free of the fear of annihilation by weapons of mass destruction—nuclear, biological, chemical. As women gain more equality throughout the world, and more control over their own childbearing processes, the population problem will ease. Birthrates will better balance with resources, thus overcoming the Malthusian "necessity" for war, famine and disease. Slowly, the development dilemma will approach satisfactory resolution. As we trade the conquest of nature for environmental housekeeping we will rid our planet of energy shortages, natural resources depletion, and chemical pollution.

There will be more openness and trust in woman-man relations, in our families and our communities. With a social structure based *on linking* instead of ranking institutions we will become less hierarchical, allowing for diversity and flexibility; and many new institutions will be more global, as the consciousness of our connectedness with one another and our environment firmly takes hold. The economic order will be drastically reshaped; caring for others will be a most highly valued and rewarded activity; and the corporate form of profit- and nonprofit-making organizations will find new and constructive roles in the overall enhancement of life and enrichment of being on the planet.

Some Key Economic Assumptions

Some desirable characteristics of a restructured economic system were described above. Yet it is well known that what is desirable is not necessarily what we bring into being; the latter tends to depend upon deep underlying assumptions. If there is to be fundamental change, it will require reassessment and change of some of these basic assumptions. Let us identify a few of the most important, a number of which have already been discussed in the preceding text:

Some Pathogenic Economic Assumptions

1. *Economic rationality and values are an adequate and appropriate guide to social decision making.* These are the most common ways by which decisions are justified, in either the public or private sector. Yet the consequences are consistently deleterious.
   a. Discounting the future at a rate comparable with prevailing interest rates is a reasonable thing to do.
   b. Becoming a debtor society (substituting credit for cash, loans for equity; deficit budgeting) in recent decades is a natural evolution.
   c. Loaning money at what were once considered "usurious" rates of interest is not a problem once our religious scruples are set aside.
   d. It is reasonable and legitimate that the absentee owners of large corporations (shareholders, takeover barons) should exert commanding influence on management decisions to insure maximum return on their investment. (Only recently have employees begun to note that they are investing their lives, while the "owners" only invest money. As one European worker put it, quoted in Hazel Henderson's *The Politics of the Solar Age*, "We are going to repeal the Divine Right of Capital, because it's just as arbitrary as was the Divine Right of Kings.")
   e. Financial speculation, non-reusable containers, extravagant packaging and advertising add to the GNP and strengthen the economy (create jobs). On the other hand, providing good education for all, beautification of the environment, providing citizen protection in urban environments are included in public-sector expenditures and represent drains on the economy.

2. *There is no reason to expect a change in the trend toward more and more of human activity being monetized and included in the mainstream economy.*
   a. Economic growth must continue (i.e. consumption of goods and services must continue to rise at an exponential rate) to create jobs.
   b. To that end it is reasonable to promote superfluous production and consumption; to see economic benefits in high "national security" expenditures; to see benefit in an ever-growing "financial industry" which contributes nothing in terms of basic goods and services, but contributes to the GNP and creates jobs.
3. *The economic problem is the existence of scarcity: Human wants are virtually infinite, but resources—labor, land, natural resources, machines—are limited.* The individual has an essentially unlimited appetite for material goods and services (including play, which translates into "leisure industries"); this appetite can be stimulated by advertising and consumer education.
4. *In general, the individual will seek to avoid work (labor); work is essentially a* means *through which one reaches consumption and leisure.* Work is an unpleasant, burdensome activity that is only engaged in for the material rewards it produces.
   a. The primary purpose of work is economic.
   b. The primary function of education is to prepare one for a job or profession.
   c. Technological progress has as one of its more important fruits that work is increasingly performed by machines.

Some Counter Assumptions

1. *Values that are adequate to guide human society are implicit in the view that we are essentially spiritual beings in a spiritual universe.* Rational analysis will continue to play a role in guiding societal decisions, supplemented by intuitive insight and consensus based on partnership rather than adversary assumptions. Sound decisions require a whole-system view, an assumption of unity with and concern for other parts of society, future generations, the Earth and its creatures.
2. *There is an important place for sub-economies and for limiting the growth of the mainstream economy.* The partial destructuring of the single global economy, and the fostering of community-

based economy, appear to be essential for the emergence and flowering of other desirable aspects of human society.

3. *Humans ultimately seek meaning, not comfort; creative work, not inactivity.* The human problem is not the existence of scarcity but the realization of abundance. Human material wants are largely learned; they are not unlimited. Material craving is an unsuccessful search for meaning.

4. *Creative work is necessary for psychological and spiritual growth.* Work is not means by which one finds fulfillment through material acquisition and trivialized leisure; creative work (including learning and leisure) is both means and end, and the closest anyone has ever come to defining the meaning of life.

Summary of System-change Features

We have argued that a fundamental system change is both desirable and plausible—desirable if it leads to the global problems becoming resolvable, and plausible because the forces to bring it about are already visible and growing. Let us summarize some of its salient characteristics:

Characteristics of an Ultimate System-change Resolution

1. *A more adequate worldview.* The Western cultural bias, and the scientific worldview which emerged out of it, are seen to be incompatible in the end with a viable future for human society. The emerging worldview is influenced by an expanded concept of science, the feminist movement, the "Green" and deep ecology movements, the renaissance of Native American and other indigenous peoples' culture, Eastern meditative traditions, new concepts in organization management, and other forces. It involves transformed ways of relating to our deeper selves, to others, and to the Earth, and a new sense of the human venture—its transcendent goals and its deep meanings.

2. *New value emphases,* based on a better picture of ourselves and the universe. The materialistic, hedonistic, dominator goals of modern societies need to be replaced by goals that have more to do with human learning and development, and with the noblest of human virtues. Ethics of the world community need to emphasize our mutual interdependence; future-oriented

decision making; fairness in distribution of natural and created wealth; economic cooperation and mutual solidarity between nations; worldwide political democracy; cherishing and preservation of diversity; and fostering a caring relationship with the Earth and all her creatures.

3. *Reconstruction of the world's economic system*, emphasizing truth-telling about the nonviable assumptions underlying the present system, and encouragement of decentralized experiments and alternative economic thinking.

4. *Assertion of a new constructive role for business.* Business is the dominant institution in modern society. Business' orientation is global: customers, sourcing, finance, marketing, competition. No other part of our society has such a global focus. Two observations relate to that fact. Business is implicated in contributing to all of the global dilemmas that now face humanity on planet Earth. On the other hand, by transforming itself and fundamentally changing the way it does business, the corporate sector can be one of the most powerful positive forces for constructive change.

Something of the flavor of the "new paradigm" business organization may be conveyed by the following table:

Some Characteristics of the Traditional and Emerging Contexts for Business*

Traditional Ways	Emerging New Trends
A. Goals	
Financial return to shareholders; contribution to society	Satisfaction of needs, fulfillment for co-workers, shareholders, customers
Goal setting through intentionality	Goal setting through insight, listening
B. Management/Leadership	
Controlling, firm control	Evoking, based on confidence
Motivate, manipulate employees	Inspire, care for teammates
'Management by objectives'	Attention to objectives and process
Rigid bureaucracy	Flexible, adaptive methodology
Focus on organizational needs	Focus on customer, stakeholder needs
Power of money, status, information	Power of awareness, insight
Leader as a status-filled role	Leader as a service-filled role
Competitive/secretive	Competitive/cooperative
Politics played	No politics

Traditional Ways	Emerging New Trends
B. Management/Leadership cont'd.	
Co-dependency/dependency	Inter-dependency
Alignment by edict	Alignment around common understandings
Emphasis on job description	Emphasis on shared responsibility
Focus on job performance	Focus includes individuals' well-being
People valued for 'productivity'	People valued for overall contribution
Dealing with conditions	Discovering context
Economics take priority	Empowerment of others important
Seeking usefulness, functionality	Seeking meaning, value as well
C. Attitude/Culture	
Solving problems	Creating opportunities
Progress by increments	Progress by leaps
Blame for failure	Support for learning from failure
Short-term focus	Long-term considerations
Technology/capital based	People and knowledge based
Linear/logical, analyzing	Creative, synthesizing
Emphasis on quantity	Emphasis on quality
Emphasis on the 'right' way	Learning, exploring, open
Calculating, manipulative	Unfolding, evolutionary
Exploitive	Socially responsible
Under time and task pressures	Knowing what is important
Emphasis on knowledge, having the answer	Emphasis on being open, questioning
D. Structure	
Fixed structure	Open, organic structure
Status-laden, rigid hierarchy	Functional, adaptive hierarchy
Power residing in management	Self-management
Past regimen reinforced	Creativity and freedom nurtured
Centralized offices, tight controls	Decentralized, local autonomy
E. Individual	
Loyal/obligated to organization	Loyal to self, to one's own purpose
Driven by survival needs	Motivated by desire to grow
Fearful and insecure	Trusting and secure
Financially motivated	Motivated by personal satisfaction
Outer acknowledgment needed	Acknowledgment comes from self
Individual 'specialness', heroics	Individual uniqueness
Adversarial, competitive thinking	Cooperative, ecological thinking
Goals are to succeed, 'get ahead'	Goals are to have integrity, feel alive
Feelings unexpressed	Okay to express feelings

* Adapted from John Renesch, Managing Director, World Business Academy, Burlingame, CA

Chapter 5

The Dynamic Processes
of Social Change

The arguments of the four preceding chapters suggest that the intensifying global problems require for their solution a fundamental change in industrialized society, and that social forces have spontaneously arisen that seem to be pushing in the direction of that change. Still unanswered, however, are such questions as how societal change takes place, whether rational actions can be effective in bringing it about, and whether a relatively smooth and nondisruptive fundamental change is even possible.

On these questions there has not been a great deal of agreement among scholars. They have argued long and hard about how social change occurs—what are the roles of leadership, planned interventions, significant events, conflicts between classes, historical cycles, and revolutionary movements. Major change can be triggered by catastrophe, by charismatic heroes, by a newly awakening public—but what are the conditions under which the trigger will actually result in lasting change? Despite the fact that no real consensus exists on the theory of social change, there are some key ideas that seem fruitful to consider in terms of interpreting contemporary signs of change.

The Nature of Societal Change

The view of change reflected in much journalism is tempting but misleading. Journalism seeks to understand the present by finding in earlier events the "causes" of the present situation—policy changes made by the early Reagan administration, the OPEC oil crisis, the aftermath of the Vietnam war. Yet it is clear that still earlier occurrences also affect the present and the future—things like the Great Depression of the 1930s, the Industrial Revolution, the Copernican revolution.

Furthermore, such a cultural shift as the Copernican revolution is not a simple change of mind. Such fundamental change in the way people perceive, value, behave, and relate typically takes place when awareness, intention, and action come together in concrete situations that affect their lives directly. The Copernican shift which we now perceive as the transition from medieval to modern thinking was not a simple dissemination of some new ideas from Copernicus and Galileo to the masses. It was a disorderly process, involving vast numbers of individuals and small groups freeing themselves from an old mind-set and struggling to a new awareness. This was accompanied by much discomfort and by social movements, some of which were as nonconformist as any that appeared during the 1960s. The new worldview set in motion new patterns of social and institutional changes which are still playing themselves out.

Social change comes about as people resolve problems and meet challenges, discovering new processes of seeing, thinking, and being. Change is rooted in experience and reflected in the consciousness of people. To whatever extent societal change can be consciously nurtured and guided toward the highest ideals and values, it will be mainly through understanding the process and finding ways to support individuals, organizations, and popular movements that seem to reflect the desired ideals and values.

Society is best understood as a whole, organic system. We mentioned earlier the phenomenon of self-healing in living systems: An ecosystem, in the process of healing itself after a forest fire, changes to a different kind of place; the human body forges new neural pathways after a stroke; individuals manage to become functioning adults despite adverse childhood conditions. In all such examples, the change process exhibits goal-directed activity, organic continuity, and the palpable concreteness of the factors influencing change.

The organicity and wholeness of the societal change in which we are immersed is obscured in various ways, of which five are mentioned below. As a result, people tend to adopt simplistic views of social change—hence to have unrealistic expectations for what might be accomplished by a piece of legislation, political action, or technological and managerial interventions.

Complexity. The first of the ways in which the wholeness of change is obscured is simply by the extreme complexity of the system, and the fact that the individual's view is limited to such a small part of the whole. Our attention is repeatedly drawn to the specific parts—

the price of bread, the cars on the freeway at rush hour, the politician's campaign speech. The fluidity and overlapping realities of complex patterns, the interconnectedness and feedback paths, are abstract and less apparent. Because of our partial and biased view, we are surprised by "unintended consequences" of legislative action, or we find that the racial bias that is supposedly eliminated by "affirmative action" reappears in some more subtle form.

Tendency toward a short-term focus. It is difficult to appreciate the distant origins or the long-term consequences of contemporary events if one's focus is always on the short term and the immediately controllable. Partly this tendency is cultural. In modern society we are habituated to the brief news item, the disparaging of that which is not the latest style, the action that is to be taken tomorrow. In part it has been built into system incentives—the economic convention of discounting the future at a rate comparable with interest rates; the shift from investment to speculation in the securities market, which puts pressure on corporate management to focus on short-term financial return; the two-year term of Congresspersons, who are consequently always running for re-election.

This trait may even be biological in its origins. A recent book *New World, New Mind* (Ornstein and Ehrlich, 1988) argues that human beings were shaped by evolutionary forces that predispose us to respond to immediate stimuli and to seek short-term success.

Psychological blocks to truth-seeing. Thirdly, there are strong psychological resistances to accurate perception. Individuals have a well-known ability to not see what would be psychologically disturbing. It is a fact, for example, that at projected rates of use, the Earth's supply of fossil fuels will be essentially gone in a few generations. There are no projected safe sources of abundant, cheap energy. Furthermore, the economy has become so dependent on cheap energy that any departure from the energy binge would amount to a major restructuring. Add to this that the burning of fossil fuels is the major contributor to the notorious "greenhouse effect" on the Earth's climate. Yet the prospect of any serious effort to markedly reduce energy usage is literally "unthinkable." The economic incentives that affect energy use still amount to a de facto policy of "burn it up fast!"

Dualistic thinking. A fourth element in the veil that obscures perception of the social change process is the Western pattern of dualistic thinking. Conflict is habitually seen, not as an interactive aspect of change, but as opposition: conservative versus liberal; communist versus capitalist; humanist versus religionist. When both "sides" characterize the "other" as opponent, they fail to appreciate their dependence on one another. The peace movements, for instance, put forth a needed critique of a runaway nuclear arms race, possibly a consummately patriotic action; yet they were often branded by the militarists as disloyal.

Social movements such as those described in Chapter 3 are not always comfortable to have around, and their behavior is not always virtuous. Yet the characterization of social movements as "protest" movements, somehow outside the mainstream of opinion, has tended to get in the way of understanding how such movements are often indicators of what changes the future requires, and a vital part of the process of change.

Cultural bias. Cultures too have perceptual blocks, and see different realities. From some perceptions this fifth element may include all others. We are all culturally "hypnotized" in the sense that all of our lives we have accepted suggestions from our surroundings as to how we should perceive reality, and we perceive as our culture has taught us. Native American Indians, for example, perceive everything in the universe as alive, and interrelated; thus their attitudes toward complexity or toward taking care of the Earth and its creatures are far different from those of modern, industrialized society. People have been reluctant to recognize this "cultural hypnosis" even though it has been pointed out by many well-known figures from Plato to Ouspensky.

Thomas Berry (1988) writes of how the unquestioned desirability of technological advance and economic growth was so much a part of our "consensus trance" that when the book *The Limits to Growth* was published pointing out the long-term folly of continued exponential growth, "a general outcry could be heard across the country. That outcry was more than a justified criticism of the specific data or the time scale of future events. It was resentment against the indication that the dynamism of our consumer society was the supreme pathology of all history."

It has been suggested (in Chapter 2) that the contemporary melange of global problems and destabilizing forces may be essentially irresolvable within the frameworks of prevailing meanings and perceptions. These frameworks may themselves be root causes of many problems and may prevent us from seeing others more clearly and simply.

The Dynamics of Social Change

In general, there appear in history two kinds of change with significantly different dynamics. We could call them *ordinary* change, within a basic pattern or paradigm that exhibits continuity, and *transformational* change, which involves a shift in the basic underlying assumptions or core paradigm. Great social advances made through legislation in the past two centuries are an example of "ordinary" change. Profound impacts on our way of life, stemming from technological advances since the Industrial Revolution, would also probably be considered examples of ordinary societal change. The total shift in worldview associated with the Copernican revolution, on the other hand, was so revolutionary that this is typically taken as the supreme example of paradigmatic or transformational change.

Precipitators of change. Physical or cultural whole-system challenges are among the pressures which precipitate change. There may be a human-caused or natural disaster which demands such total commitment that old ways of being and doing are cast aside in an attempt to relieve human misery or heal a natural system. The precipitating factor can be a spreading awareness that something must be done to rectify an unsatisfactory condition. New technology (for example, mechanization of cloth making, or, more recently, nuclear weapons), or new understandings of reality (such as evolutionary theory), can overturn traditional ways and leave people with a sense of alienation.

Theorists of revolutionary change (for example, Davies, 1971) make use of the concept of "dissynchronization." This is an elaboration on the "self-healing" concept mentioned in the Introduction. Societies, like biological organisms, have a capacity for self-healing and self-regulation. That is to say, the society has a built-in tendency to maintain consistency among prevailing beliefs and values, the environment, and the social structure. If one of these three aspects changes, the natural tendency is for the others to maintain a kind of synchronization. (An example would be the social, legal, demographic, and cultural changes that took place with gradual industrialization of the United States.) However, on occasion one of these aspects may get too far "out of step" with the others—as when the rising aspirations among the people of India collided with the realities of British imperialist policy. This creates the possibility of revolutionary or transformational change, as people in large numbers are motivated to seek a new dynamic equilibrium.

An example of societal change. Societies generally attempt to solve their problems by "ordinary" change. The pattern typically starts with a shift in *awareness*. In the case of environmental degradation, the impacts of industrial society on the environment had been worsening for generations. However, the catalyst which got things moving was Rachel Carson's book *Silent Spring* (1962), sounding the alert with regard to the chemical poisoning of the land and its consequences. This triggered a *reassessment* in which environmental issues arrived on the political agenda. There followed various forms of *action* by citizen groups which in the U.S. resulted in legislation and creation of an Environmental Protection Agency. There then was a period of *reflection*, of evaluating whether the action would prove appropriate and sufficient.

The cycle of "ordinary" change may repeat many times. However, it may eventually arrive at an awareness that more fundamental change is required. In the environmental example, increasingly people came to conclude that legislation alone will not solve the problem; deeper level change of the "transformational" sort is required.

It is this second kind of change that particularly concerns us. If indeed modern Westernized society is encountering fundamental challenges to its basic, underlying assumptions, the characteristics of "transformational" change are especially pertinent.

Social movements as a force for change. Social movements are often a significant factor in "ordinary" change and almost always a major factor in "transformational" change. They typically play a role in raising awareness of inequities or undesirable conditions, and in getting the issue of a need for change on the political agenda. They provide access to participation, and may be vehicles for ethical action. And they constitute a community for creating alternatives and for evaluating progress.

Throughout history nonviolent social movements have been important in changing social conditions and policies, typically against the will of powerful and even oppressive governments. They have been the primary means for people to experience and express their power in bringing about positive social change. Recent decades have witnessed the influence of many such movements—civil rights; anti-Vietnam War; women's; anti-nuclear; peace and democratic people's movements around the world, in the Philippines, South Africa, Eastern Europe.

The most successful social movements are processes in which the general public is alerted, educated, and mobilized to participate directly in resolving a social problem and bringing conditions more into alignment with widely accepted human values and principles, despite varying degrees of opposition from the institutional power holders. Such social movements simultaneously contribute to desirable social change, promote participatory democracy, and help restore core values and sensibilities to the center of the society's decision-making process and institutions.

While social movement activists and organizations are crucial catalysts, they are not the real force that brings about change. That force is the general population. Social change happens when the general public reacts strongly to specific problems or more general system malfunctioning. The real constituency of social movements, then, is not the official power holders, but the general population. Throughout the history of the democracies in North America and Europe, in particular, social movements have provided the crucial means by which the people have been able to counteract the influence of powerful entrenched elites and special-interest groups.

The perception of legitimacy. A key concept is that of the *legitimacy* of institutions and institutional behaviors. Political power and the institution of public policy ultimately require the consent of the public, which is to say, the public's perception of their legitimacy. The official powerholders in any society have that power only as long as they are perceived as the legitimate caretakers of the society's basic moral beliefs and values. (This is not to deny, of course, that government by forceful imposition of power can exist for periods that are, in a historical sense, temporary.)

The general population usually acquiesces to society's powerholders and institutions as long as they seem to be carrying out the interests of the whole society in an agreed upon fair and ethical manner. The legitimated role of the powerholders, in other words, is to carry out the general will of the people and to oversee the general welfare of the whole society. It is expected that they will not give special benefits to themselves or a set of privileged people or groups. This understanding of the role of the powerholders constitutes a *compact* with the people. As long as the people believe that this pact is being honored, they will in general abide by the leadership and the institutions that the powerholders control.

This power of the people to legitimatize authority, and to withdraw legitimacy, we find to be, throughout history, the most powerful of forces for transformational social change. (This was demonstrated most recently in Eastern Europe; playwright Vaclav Havel, hero of the 1989 Czechoslovakian transformation, described it as "the power of the powerless.") In a democracy, where citizen involvement is prized and anticipated, this cycle of public consent, and withdrawal of that consent, is part of the normal political process. Public policy is influenced by a wide variety of citizen actions, including nonviolent social movements, special interest group advocacy, labor unions, community self-help groups, and traditional party politics. In other forms of government this process may be much more chaotic; in severely oppressive situations it may take the form of violent revolution.

The 1989 responses in China and in Eastern Europe to the rising demand for liberty and democracy provide a fascinating comparison in this regard. China had made considerable headway, since the 1949 revolution, with regard to some social problems, such as starvation. Yet, overall, many problems remain. The repeated failures of policies, and of clusters of policies, suggest that some sort of whole-system change will be required to make the problems solvable. Such whole-system change is almost never led from the top; there is too much interest vested in maintaining the existing system. Instead, the force for fundamental change comes typically from a middle-band of people who are not totally focused on the necessities for mere survival, yet on the other hand are not too invested in maintaining the status quo. In modern societies they may be a fairly well-educated, high-competence group (like the Chinese students). The real challenge to the leadership is to allow the necessary system change to take place in a nonviolent, nondisruptive way—a challenge the Chinese leadership did not meet in the spring of 1989. In Eastern Europe, on the other hand, there was adequate appreciation of the ineluctability of fundamental change that leadership, by and large, made a more constructive response.

The Problem of Social Change in a Democracy

It is important to grasp how basically this matter of transformational social change interacts with the concepts of democracy and free enterprise. In the course of their activities the various elements of society—individuals, groups, corporations, government agencies—make what we may term *microdecisions* (for example, to buy a certain product, to employ a person for a particular task, to develop and market a new product, to enact a piece of legislation). These microdecisions interact and lead to *macrodecisions* affecting the entire society and the world (for example, price and wage levels, a 3 percent annual growth rate in energy usage, public and private debt exceeding 10 trillion dollars, deterioration of the central cities, pollution of the environment, depletion of nonrenewable resources). *The problem today is that microdecisions which are perfectly reasonable, by all the criteria that have governed in the past, are currently adding up to unsatisfactory macrodecisions. In the broadest sense, this constitutes the fundamental dilemma of contemporary society. To recognize this is to stop searching for someone to blame, and to start searching for the sorts of changes that would make the process become workable again.*

Adam Smith, in *The Wealth of Nations*, justified capitalism by claiming that when the entrepreneur "intends only his own gain … he is … led by an invisible hand to promote an end which was no part of his intention.… By pursuing his own interest he frequently promotes that of the society more effectually than when he really intends to promote it." By now we know *the reverse may also be true*. In the absence of consensus on the overarching values and goals that also guide the microdecisions, individuals and organizations often choose on the basis of their own short-term, imprudent self-interest, and the consequent macrodecisions can be results desired by no one.

It would appear that the invisible hand needs a little help these days. Such help has existed for years in the form of government control via antitrust laws, commerce regulations, Keynesian manipulations of the money supply and interest rates, incentives to reduce air pollution, and so on. Yet the dilemma worsens.

The fundamental problem is not simply a matter of tradeoffs—it is that the tradeoffs seem to grow steadily more intolerable. As one cartoon caption put it a number of years ago: "There's a pricetag on everything. You want a high standard of living, you settle for a low quality of life."

An obvious solution would seem to be to select desired macrodecisions and derive microdecisions from them. The logic is appealing. It would appear to be possible to choose appropriate national and planetary goals that are in accord with the best available knowledge regarding human fulfillment, and then determine what kinds of microdecisions would be necessary to achieve those goals.

But there is a catch. The *means* used to achieve those individual actions have to be compatible with the ends. In a democratic society one cannot dictate goals—even desirable ones. There is no set of paramount objectives that, once chosen, unambiguously guides the actions of society. Rather, there are sets of goals, often mutually inconsistent or partially conflicting (for example, local decision making, energy self-sufficiency, environmental protection, economic growth, positive incentives where feasible, private sector action preferred to public sector actions where feasible). The macrodecision delineating the priority to be attached to each goal varies with time and is a matter of what wins out in the political process; there is no timeless set of priorities. The microdecisions necessary to actualize the chosen goals have to be guided primarily by an understanding of the linkages between them. Forcing correct microdecisions by coercive decrees or behavior manipulation is obviously incompatible with basic democratic principles.

At this point in history, for suitable macrodecisions to be made requires *a collective and voluntary redirection of the whole society*. These long-term goals must be chosen in a democratic political process. Successful implementation of a new selection of macrodecisions calls for re-education of the whole society so that people understand the implications of the macrodecisions and can make their own individual microdecisions accordingly. It also requires institutional changes for effectively employing widespread citizen participation at local, regional, national, and global levels. Nothing less than this sort of cultural and institutional change will resolve the dilemma of managing an increasingly complex society without sacrificing liberty.

An Example of "Grand Theory" Societal Change

One "grand theory" of social change is sufficiently apposite to the present world situation as to merit our attention here. It is to be found in the writings of Pitirim Sorokin.

Sorokin founded the Department of Sociology at Harvard University in 1930. His first-hand experience of the calamities of war, revolution, and totalitarianism (in Russia) led him to search for the deeper patterns that lay beneath such events. He studied a wide range of social and cultural indicators for as far back in Western history as there were any records, and to a considerable extent in other cultures as well. From a grand synthesis of all of these separate threads, he developed a theory that forecast a fairly imminent decline in the influence of what he termed "post-medieval Western sensate culture," involving a profound crisis in meaning and values. Western society, he argued, would be faced with the choice of either going through a "transformation" in its basic meaning-and-value structure, or else proceeding toward some form of degeneration and self-destruction. He was essentially optimistic that the path of transformation would be carried off successfully, but warned that it was by no means a sure thing. (Sorokin, 1941)

Essentially, Sorokin's analysis disclosed that much of history fits a pattern of cyclical rise and fall of two basic value systems which he termed "ideational" (spiritually or religiously oriented) and "sensate" (materialistic). The ideational value system sees true reality as lying beyond the material world perceptible to the physical senses. It is to be found in the spiritual realm, and can be known only through personal revelation or other forms of inner experience. This value system subscribes to absolute legal and ethical standards, and to ideas of truth and beauty that stem from the super-rational realm. Ideational values were dominant in Western society between about the fifth and the tenth centuries, and comparable periods can be found in other cultures such as the Hindu, the Hellenic, and the Buddhist.

The sensate culture, on the other hand, rests on the belief that only what can be perceived with the senses, namely matter-energy in its various forms, has any reality. All laws and ethical values are relative and are based on utilitarian, empirical considerations. Such a value system tends to be poor in philosophy and art, but rich in positivistic scientific and technological achievements. In the West, sensate values have been in the ascendant since about the French Revolution. Parallels can be found in the late Egyptian civilization and in the last centuries of Hellenic civilization preceding 500 C.E.

A third value system, the "integral," has appeared relatively briefly at various times in history; it represents a harmonious blending of spiritual and sensory values, and more or less describes the finest flowering of any culture. In the West, this period occupied the years approximately 1500 to 1800 and includes the period in Western European history known as the Enlightenment.

Sorokin's analysis (written over half a century ago) further indicated that the sensate period would shortly come to an end, and that this would be accompanied by a breakdown of industrial culture. This was not necessarily a pessimistic forecast; Sorokin saw a high probability that out of the disintegrating sensate culture would arise a new transcendental worldview that could be the foundation of a new integral value system. He saw the most constructive activity the society could undertake to be study and application of the "techniques of altruistic transformation"—that is, increasing the world's supply of creative, unselfish love.

It was easy for sophisticated people to dismiss Sorokin, either because the end of industrial culture was so threatening to contemplate, or because "creative altruism" seemed such a "soft" concept. Nevertheless, over the half century since his *Dynamics* was published, his work seems increasingly more pertinent.

The Real Challenge

We can summarize the argument. The reasons for taking seriously a scenario in which the industrialized world has entered a transition period shifting toward a "trans-industrial" culture are 1) the global problems appear to be unsolvable in the framework of the industrial order; 2) an assortment of social movements are pulling society toward a new vision; 3) it is becoming clear that that new direction is essentially the direction needed to make the problems resolvable; and 4) people are liberating themselves from old constraints and recognizing both their external power, in their ability to change institutions through their power to define legitimacy, and their internal power, in the sense of drawing on inner resources which had heretofore not been recognized.

Nothing in history suggests that such a transition is likely to be smooth; to the contrary, it seems more likely to be characterized by social and political disruption and widespread human misery. The underlying cause of the disruptiveness and misery, however, is fear. Perhaps these aspects of change can be mitigated or even largely eliminated if fear and anxiety levels can be kept down, through raising the level of understanding about the necessity of transition at this point in history.

In short, if our analysis is correct and industrialized society is in a period of fundamental transition, there is little that might be done to change that. The momentum is already gathering, and whatever transformation is to take place, will. What *is* undetermined is how rough the passage will be. It is here our greatest challenge lies. Can accurate understanding of the necessary transition be disseminated so that people will be exhilarated by the opportunities, rather than alarmed by the uncertainties? It is here that business, because of its dominant position in the society, can potentially make the greatest contribution.

Chapter 6

The New Creative Role
of Business

The whole point of understanding is to enable one to act. We now turn to the question: *So what?* As a business executive, suppose I am convinced that the picture presented here is more or less accurate, what should I do? The brief answer is 1) Survive; 2) Prosper; and 3) Contribute.

A little less succinctly:

1. Understand the transition period we are in, so that actions will lead to survival. In a period of rapid change, the things that will contribute to survivability of the organization are quite different from the behaviors that worked in a more stable environment. Also it is important, in such stressful times, to do those things which will contribute to one's own healthy survival—physically, psychologically, spiritually.

2. Prosper, in the sense of the dictionary meaning: to succeed in an enterprise; to be strong and flourishing. Not as an end in itself, but in order to be able to contribute. To prosper in the highly competitive environment just ahead, a corporation will have to attract and hold the most competent and creative people. These persons are not responding to the same allurements that were effective a decade or two ago. They demand a very different kind of work environment, one that will provide freedom and encouragement to "be all that they can be."

3. The best people are demanding of their employers more responsible planetary citizenship. Since the world is in trouble, this implies contributing to the resolution of the global problems—not as a charitable institution, or by getting deeply involved with non-business activities, *but by doing business*

differently. In addition to this, when business leaders communicate their understanding of the need for creative transformation, because of their influential position in society they contribute to lowering anxiety, and hence to the likelihood of a smooth transition.

Let us try to be more explicit about each of those.

Understanding and Surviving

Thriving on Chaos is the title chosen by Tom Peters (1987) for his book on what he sees as a "management revolution." Although the "revolution" he describes is mild compared with the sea change we are talking about here, the phrase is an apt one to describe the challenge. Surviving and prospering in a chaotic environment is precisely what the game is going to be about for the next couple of decades. During this transition period timing will be critical. The situation is a little bit like riding a surfboard. If you fall behind the wave of change, or misjudge it, you're in trouble. On the other hand, if you sense the direction of change and try to get ahead of the wave, you may court another kind of disaster.

Failures of the present paradigm. Summarizing some of what has gone before, we note that the capitalist version of the Western industrial paradigm has achieved some remarkable successes. However, in the end *it seems unable to find a satisfactory resolution to three fundamental flaws:*

- It fails to meet the basic condition that every citizen have the opportunity to be a full and valued participant, with the feeling of belonging and being useful.
- It fails to achieve a synergism of individual and organizational microdecisions (for example, what appliances to purchase, what products to market) such that the resultant societal macrodecisions (such as how serious a "greenhouse effect" will ensue) are satisfactory even to those who made the component decisions.
- It fails to achieve, over the long term, a satisfactorily equitable distribution of power and wealth.

The socialist version of the paradigm aimed at being a corrective to the first and third of these flaws; planned society to the second. It is now clear that these alternative versions simply lead to a mix of the same problems in different proportions.

Perhaps most seriously, *all versions of the modern paradigm fail to give the contemporary person the sense of being a useful and necessary member of a social whole which in turn is geared into a meaningful plan of existence within the totality of a cosmic or divine order.* In the long run, that is a potentially fatal flaw.

But however real may be the problems of the world and the failures of the past, a negative problem-focused obsession is not the most desirable basis for decision and action. The great achievements of industry and technology, of private enterprise and democracy, did not come about through focusing on the negative conditions from which humans were attempting to escape, but rather through an entrepreneurial response to the vision and the challenge of making things better. Similarly, the best reason for involvement with issues of global development is the positive challenge of creating a better world than the one we have known.

Toward a trans-industrial "learning society." The positive challenge we are suggesting is of modern society in transition to some sort of trans-industrial "learning society." Among the characteristics of such a society would be:

- Work as life enhancement and fulfillment—beyond the concept of work as a commodity traded on the labor markets.
- Corporate management deriving its power of authority from the consent of all those stakeholders whose lives are affected by the corporation's activities, particularly those who invest their lives and/or money to significant extent—less subservience to the goals of absentee financial investors.
- Various flourishing informal alternative economies—thinking globally; acting both globally and locally—with a good fraction of exchange taking place outside the mainstream economy while large corporations continue to gain global dimensions.
- Worldwide cooperation toward global development with clear targets, but encouraging a wide diversity of alternative development paths for different societies—with a far greater role being played by grassroots individual initiative as compared with technical expertise and the policies of financial institutions.
- Promotion of integrity, creativity, trust, and cooperation—beyond vicious competition, pressure, manipulation, and deceit.
- Reduction of bureaucracy in large organizations—beyond the concept of "trust is good; control is better."

- Recognition of the important roles for nonprofit and voluntary organizations, small business—beyond the concepts "big business can do it; government can fix it."
- Values and incentives that foster care of the Earth: its life-support processes, its resources, its wildernesses, and its beauty—beyond the concept of the Earth as subject to human desires.
- Worldwide consensus and cooperative action toward establishing the Rule of Law, and assuring the rights delineated in the Universal Declaration of Human Rights, throughout the world—beyond national egotism and despotism.
- Appreciation and respect for the foundations of society: the mothers, children, and families—without whom all the rest would become meaningless.

However, things could move significantly in most or even all of these directions, and yet the business sector and society not be transformed in the sense we are describing. Especially in a time when the adjective "new-paradigm" is being applied very loosely to business organizations and educational seminars, it is important to distinguish between improvements to the existing system, however major, and a fundamental change of paradigm. *The hallmark of the latter is a shift in the underlying assumptions about the nature of ourselves and the universe.*

Understanding the shifting view of reality. Both capitalist and socialist forms of modern Western society arise from essentially the same view of reality—the one stemming from nineteenth-century European male-dominated science (which in turn has roots much further back, in medieval Christianity). This is a view which emphasizes separateness and thing-ness, and seeks explanations in terms of elemental phenomena (such as collision of fundamental particles, chemical structure of DNA, random mutations of genetic material).

The fact that this view is now challenged gives a hint as to how all-pervasive a shift is really taking place. By the latter part of the twentieth century it has become apparent to a large and widening group of people that, however successful science might be in providing the power to predict and control in the physical (and to some extent the biological) world, it has had a serious negative influence on our understanding of values. Its effect was to undermine the common religious base of values and to replace it with a form of moral relativism. Into the vacuum came, as "pseudovalues," economic and technical attributes, such as material progress, efficiency, productivity. Decisions that would affect the lives of people around the globe for generations to come were made on the basis of short-term economic considerations. The "technological imperative" to develop and apply any technology that could turn a profit or destroy an enemy came to endanger both the life-support systems of the planet and human civilization.

Now this is all showing signs of changing. Society appears to be restructuring itself, basing itself on a different picture of reality. Nothing could be more important than the deepest possible understanding of the new reality base, and its implications.

Over the past three decades in particular there has been rapidly increasing interest in the religious philosophies of the East, in becoming aware of the resplendent dimensions of the self, and in the "perennial wisdom" that is claimed to lie at the heart of all of the world's spiritual traditions. "Becoming aware of the self" may not seem very appealing to the action-focused businessperson, but that is because we miss the point. There is nothing in the concept of "enlightenment" that is in any way antithetical to leading a very active life; it only has to do with the question: To what end are you active?

Not only is this inner wisdom or "primordial tradition" (Rossner, 1989) to be found in the esoteric traditions of the West and the religions of the East, it is also present in the spiritual traditions of the world's indigenous peoples, although with a somewhat different emphasis. The growing interest in the traditional wisdom of such native peoples as the North American Indians is very pertinent to definition of the emerging paradigm. Whereas the traditions of the East urge one to look deeply within oneself to discover the universe, the traditions of the indigenous peoples teach looking deeply within nature to discover oneself. Together with the Western penchant toward looking deeply into that knowledge which is pragmatically useful, these three outlooks form a sort of three-legged stool. Any one of them alone is subject to extremes and abuses; together they may actually suffice to guide us in living harmoniously on a small planet.

In recent years we have seen the rise of a "new heresy." Like the "scientific heresy" of several centuries ago, it essentially amounts to a widening group of people discovering that their experienced reality is not what the established authorities have been telling them. Both in the broader society (in interest in various meditative disciplines, mind-body approaches to health care, arcane studies and religious philosophies) and in the scientific community as well, are found indications that the long-accepted tacit metaphysical assumptions of modern Western society are being re-examined. Both native nature-wisdom and the mystical insight of the East are found to highlight kinds of knowledge, aspects of human experience, that are obscured or overlooked by Western science.

The prevailing metaphysical assumption of modern science is still that the basic stuff of the universe is matter-energy. This matter-energy is found in discrete elements of quanta and elementary particles. Whatever mind or consciousness is, it emerged out of matter at the end of a long evolutionary process. Whatever can be learned about consciousness must ultimately be reconciled with the kind of knowledge we get from studying the physical processes of the brain.

In contrast, the basic metaphysical assumption implied in the "primordial tradition" is that the universe is a connected whole. Its fundamental stuff is consciousness: Mind or consciousness is primary, and matter-energy emerges out of universal mind. Although the things of the world may appear superficially separate, at a deeper level they are connected. Individual minds are not separated (although individual brains appear to be); they connect at some level not accessible to ordinary conscious awareness. Ultimately reality is contacted, not through the physical sciences, but through the deep intuition. Consciousness is not the end-product of material evolution; rather, consciousness is original cause. Because of the way in which our unconsciously held beliefs influence our perceptions, it is less accurate to say, "I'll believe it when I see it," than to observe that "I'll see it when I believe it."

It may seem quite preposterous to suggest that society might make such an extreme shift. Certainly neither mainstream science nor mainstream religion are comfortable with these assumptions presently. Of course we are not saying that these will be the new assumptions; only that there are many indications that point in that direction. The growing strength of the "New Thought" churches, such as Church of Religious Science and Unity, is only one of these; these religions have at their core essentially the assumptions described above. Furthermore, the fact that these assumptions are not incompatible with the reformulated science hypothesized in Chapter 4 contributes to the likelihood. If it turns out that something like the "primordial tradition" assumptions do prevail, the impact on all institutions of society, and on the course of history, will be as great as have been the effects of the scientific revolution.

Regardless of whether the new metaphysic can be clearly identified at this point, some fundamental transformation of modern society is almost certainly imminent. The demonstrated inadequacy of the present scientific worldview has produced an imperative. *It is impossible to create a well-working society on the base of a view of reality which is fundamentally inadequate, seriously incomplete, and mistaken in basic assumptions. Yet that is precisely what the modern world has been attempting to do.*

Putting it more bluntly, if the "perennial wisdom" comes to be seen as a complement to Western science and a summary of important and universal human experience, the whole of modern society will be restructured as a result. *If the fundamental fact about us is that we are spiritual beings in a spiritual universe and the modern denial of this is in error, then any social structure which is built around that denial will in the end fail to be satisfactory.*

If these surmises are correct and the metaphysical assumptions underlying modern society are shifting at the same deep level that they did at the time of the Scientific Revolution, then the "transmodern" society of the twenty-first century is likely to be as different from modern society as modern society is from medieval times. Anticipating the form of management and executive leadership in the twenty-first century is analogous to having forecasted the shape of the modern business organization from the mid-seventeenth century.

Yet we can be aware of the transition in a way that our seventeenth-century European counterparts could not. We can examine the forerunner changes that are already observable, and can anticipate what kind of transformation of society would result if those values and outlooks came to prevail.

The long-term evolutionary trend. The New World concepts of the nineteenth and early twentieth centuries provided inspiration for peoples around the globe. The long-term evolutionary vision represented in those goals can be fairly well summed up in three components:

1. *Increasing awareness and mastery of life* as embodied in the open inquiry of science, the application of technology to improve quality of living, and the free search for appropriate guiding beliefs and values;

2. *Liberation* as exemplified in the political ideal of personal liberty within a lawful order, the economic ideal of private enterprise, and the cultural ideal of individuation;
3. *Democratization* as exemplified in the social ideals of free education and public dissemination of scientific knowledge, the economic ideal of equal opportunity, and the political ideal of participatory democracy.

In recent decades the U.S., together with much of the rest of the industrialized world, has departed seriously from that evolutionary vision. Awareness and mastery became reduced to utilitarian science in the service of technology, and to technology in the service of mindless economic growth and inescapable militarism. Liberation stopped far short of economic and social liberation of those in the Third World who had recently achieved political liberation. (It also, until recently, failed to include women.) The effectiveness of democratic processes, and the number of functioning democratic governments in the world, declined for a while, although that trend may have been reversed in the past few years.

These three long-term evolutionary goals are still capable of inspiring the morale they once did. An image of the future which involves their fulfillment is more attractive than the heedless consumption-and-growth model that presently dominates society's decision making, and less threatening than a concept of "transform-ation" that implies voyaging into a totally uncharted future. It is this which makes the scenario of a relatively smooth, nondisruptive transfiguration of modern society more plausible than it would otherwise appear.

In brief, the single most important factor in surviving the times ahead is an accurate interpretation of what is happening, one which is continually re-examined in light of events and new information. The same can be said for prospering.

Being Excellent in a Highly Competitive Environment

Few doubt that the business environment in the near term will be not only uncertain, but highly competitive. While the global dilemmas remain unresolved, high quality of life will be a scarce commodity; individuals and countries alike will be in intense competition. Businesses face competition not only from other businesses in the same country, but, increasingly, from outside. There is an international labor market for the first time in history; jobs move as freely as sources of natural resources used to.

Yet at the same time we appear to be moving in the direction of perceiving wholeness over separateness, choosing cooperation over competition, valuing relationship over things. Internationally, the countries that compete best are characterized by a high degree of cooperation within the society. Corporations that compete best have high levels of internal cooperation. Without gainsaying the virtues of competition in a free market, it is nonetheless apparent that the future belongs to those who can preserve those virtues while creating in their organizations and in society a climate of caring, cooperativeness, richness of meaning, and quality relationships.

Attracting and holding the best people. Most of all, the competition will be keen for the most creative and flexible people. To attract and hold the most competent people in a competitive market, a company will have to offer them what they want.

Michael Maccoby's (1988) summary of our situation is current and research-based; it is worth quoting at some length:

> The global market demands that companies produce higher-quality products and services.... [Society] needs better, more cost-effective services in health, education, welfare, and law enforcement. To achieve these goals, businesses and bureaucracies must eliminate expensive levels of administration and balance control with self-management. Employees must not only work hard, but care about cutting costs and satisfying customers. New work relations require sharing knowledge and continual learning. As organizations flatten out, there will be less opportunity for promotion. The traditional incentives of hierarchy, money, status, and power will be in short supply.
>
> [There is a growing group] who do fit these demands.... These are men and women whose main goal at work is self-development. From childhood they have sharpened intellectual and interpersonal skills to succeed at work and get along with people. These self-developers are motivated to solve problems cooperatively with co-workers, customers, and clients. They are ready to learn and succeed in the new workplace, which demands a combination of technical knowledge and teamwork.
>
> But the self-developers are frustrated and turned off by bureaucratic organization and leaders who do not share their values. They resent work that does not allow them to improve their skills and maintain their marketability. They want to be free to respond individually to customers and clients, to be entrepreneurs instead of narrow specialists. They want to be

treated as whole persons, not as role performers. Yet they are wary of being swallowed up by work. Motivated to succeed in family life as well as in a career, and to balance work with play, they continually question how much of themselves to invest in the workplace.

Much business practice is still oriented around outdated theories of motivation which assume that people are motivated by money, power, status, or a hierarchy of needs. To feel whole at work, people must have a meaningful say over conditions that affect them. Ownership is not necessarily the key. Yugoslavian workers who "own" their companies and elect the managing director still can feel alienated and turned off by boring work.

What the new view implies. Roger Harrison (1983) has written with a rare combination of a rich management consulting experience and sensitivity to the profound belief-system changes taking place. He urges taking a whole-system view of business:

> Seen from a global viewpoint, the organization exists only as part of a larger reality, supported and nurtured by the larger system on which it depends: the nation, its culture, and many interest groups, the world economic and political system, and the physical and biological planet itself.... From such a viewpoint, organizational purpose is not simply decided by its members, but is in large part 'given' by its membership in the larger system....
>
> Adopting such a point of view requires a fundamental change in one's orientation to goals and to the success and failure of one's plans.... [People who] strive to succeed ... experience high stress, as can be seen from the ever-increasing popularity of alcohol, drugs, and stress management courses.... A lot of that stress comes from seeing ourselves and our organization as autonomous. We deny our dependency on larger systems and events, and then we blame ourselves when our inharmonious actions do not lead to the achievement of our goals.... We can, however, take the [alternative] view that our organization has an appropriate place in the larger system, and that our task as management and leaders is to attune our organization to its environment in order to discover what our part is and play it. The difficulties we experience are interpreted as signs and signals from the environment that we are somehow out of resonance with our true role.... According to this point of view it should not be difficult for an organization to survive and thrive, any more than an organ in a healthy body has to work especially hard to survive. When it plays its part, it receives the nourishment

it needs. From a system point of view, then, strategic thinking is a search for meaning, rather than a search for advantage.

One could hardly find a better example of advice that makes sense in the emerging paradigm, but is likely to sound like dangerous nonsense from the standpoint of the old.

We have emphasized the importance, in competitive and uncertain times, of attracting and holding the best people. One of the features the most creative individuals want in the workplace is a sense of being part of an organization that is engaged in meaningful and socially beneficial activity. These persons, in particular, are asking business whether it knows its new role on the planet.

The New Role of Business

When in the Holy Roman Empire the church was the dominant institution throughout Western Europe, it assumed a responsibility for the whole. Business is now the dominant institution on the planet: Does it have to assume a similar responsibility? If so, what does this say about the goals of business? These issues raise the most fundamental questions about what business is really about.

If together we have to have concern for, not only the individual corporation, but the whole business system, and the whole planet, the most serious of the interconnected dilemmas become part of the business of business. It is a relevant concern: how business can insure that it is contributing to the global solutions rather than to the global problems.

We must not expect to be able to identify model "new-paradigm" companies. It is too early in the transition for that. If a company tried to anticipate the wave of change fully, it might be too far ahead of the environment to survive. Nevertheless, it is helpful to point to companies that probably exemplify aspects of the emerging paradigm.

England's Scott-Bader Company employs around 500 people in the chemicals and plastics industry. It is owned by the Scott-Bader Commonwealth, an organization formed for the purpose of common stewardship. Most employees of the operating company belong to the Commonwealth and participate in formulating policy; however that is by no means required. The operating company has a normal management structure, responsible to the Commonwealth. But the goals of the company are far broader than those of most. They are summarized in the Preamble to the Constitution of the Commonwealth:

> The Commonwealth has responsibilities to the wider national and international community and is endeavoring to fulfill them by fostering a movement towards a new peaceful industrial and social order. To be a genuine alternative to welfare capitalism and state-controlled communism, such an order must be non-violent in the sense of promoting love and justice, for where love stops power begins and intimidation and violence follow. One of the main requirements for a peaceful social order is, we are convinced, an organization of work based on ... a sharing of the fruits of our labors with those less fortunate instead of working only for our private security.... We must strive to release the best in man within a free community to live up to the highest that he knows and recognize the inter-dependence of means and ends as we continue working towards a new and better society.

Employment. In Europe more than in America, business shares with government responsibility for maintaining high levels of employment. But both in business and in government, the issue typically takes the form of keeping a healthy rate of economic growth, which translates into maintaining a growing level of consumption of monetized goods and services. We have seen in Chapter 4 that this approach does not solve the problem, and in fact the issue has to be restated.

We hear much about how knowledge is becoming the main resource. While there is certainly something to this argument, it does not follow that most of the present labor force will become "knowledge workers." Instead, we are finding ourselves increasingly a two-tiered society, comprised of one group who are part of the new "knowledge society" and another group who simply can't get in. Such a society is not, in the long run, politically stable.

Small private enterprise is surely one of the important keys to a nondisruptive transition. During the two decades following the oil shocks of 1973, the Fortune 500 companies phased out a net of over 6 million jobs. During the same period, nearly four times as many new jobs were created in the U.S. by businesses with less than 100 employees.

Development. All countries are developing countries. The question: What are we developing toward? is as relevant to the rich industrialized countries as to the poorest of the developing countries, even though the set of development options and constraints may be quite different.

Because of the interconnectedness of the modern world, questions about development can only be answered within the context of some picture of a viable global future. In that picture, the development paths of the richest and most powerful nations play a central role. As we have seen, development is unlikely to be a matter of continued exponential growth of GNP; a fundamental departure from that path seems likely.

Business has a crucial role in development, however, and some companies are already taking that responsibility seriously. Anita Roddick's firm The Body Shop International makes and distributes cosmetics and health care products. It has a strong commitment to setting up trade within the Third World. Not only do they make a point of using ingredients that are grown and produced in the Third World; they also help potential suppliers set up their businesses. Whole villages in India, Africa, and South America are being supported by the profits from these enterprises. It's not charity; it's business in a different way.

Environment. Environmental degradation is driven by the system. It is inherent in the system that more consumption (with its inevitable correlates on environmental impact and resource usage) contributes to the economy, whereas taking care of the environment falls in the public sector and is a drain on the economy. Thus basic change is needed. Many companies these days are committed to observing an environmental ethic, but that alone will not be enough if their constructive actions are countered by the effects of a perverse incentive system.

Security. For all the recent talk about peace and nuclear disarmament, the powerful countries of the world have not yet faced up to an obvious fact: Since the development, during World War II, of methods of mass destruction and killing at the rate of hundreds of thousands at a time, *it is no longer possible to achieve national security through military strength.* The world must, then, move on to the next question: *How, then, are we to achieve national and global security?*

The answer is well known by analogy with the intra-national case. It is called the Rule of Law.

Basically, the Rule of Law asserts the supremacy of law as opposed to that of arbitrary power. Beyond this, its definition is no trivial thing. It is not, for instance, to be simply equated with "law and order" imposed by government; for it does not presume that all laws imposed by governments are legitimate. It demands equality before the law of all persons and classes, including government and government officials. It requires the existence of an independent judiciary and legal profession. It requires of society an attitude and spirit of legality.

India's first prime minister, Jawaharal Nehru, stated that the Rule of Law is "synonymous with the maintenance of civilized existence." The 1948 Universal Declaration of Human Rights of the United Nations states: "It is essential if man is not compelled to have recourse, as a last resort, to rebellion against tyranny and oppression, that human rights should be protected by the Rule of Law." The Preamble to Canada's Constitution Act of 1982 begins "Whereas Canada is founded upon principles that recognize the supremacy of God and the Rule of Law... "

The United States is justly proud of its tradition of the Rule of Law. Yet neither the U.S. nor any of the other powerful countries acts as though it believes in the Rule of Law for the world. (International acceptance of the Rule of Law does not imply some kind of centralized World Government, an eventuality toward which we all feel serious trepidations.)

International business, such as the airlines or telecommunications, could not function without a partial rule of law. It would be expected that business would favor acceptance of the Rule of Law simply because of the advantages of a stable environment in which to do business.

But business has been ambivalent. This has been partly through fear and low trust, and partly because the economy has come to be dependent on the nation's commitment to the military approach. Here is a clear opportunity for business to show new leadership.

The New Form of Business

The modern economic system and its component parts, such as the corporation, are constructed on the basis of a picture of reality which emphasizes the separateness of things and the competitive struggle for existence. Yet as we have seen, the culture appears to be shifting to a picture emphasizing wholeness and relationship. The kind of organization people want to be in, the kind that is compatible with the wholeness view, is one that emphasizes self-development, quality of relationships, meaningful activity, and cooperative effort. Terry Mollner (1990) has written about this as "the Third Way... after capitalism and socialism." It fits in a "relationship age" in which quality of relationship has become a high value compared with the control, possession, and distribution of objects. The "Third Way" will, so Mollner claims, do a better job than capitalism of ending poverty and economic injustice, and a better job than socialism of ending mediocrity.

Probably the best available example is the Mondragon cooperatives of northern Spain. (An even larger similar activity, the Central Union, operates within Poland.) Basically, Mondragon is an association of several hundred industrial enterprises, commercial outlets, schools, farms, and a bank, owned and managed by over 20,000 owners, who are also the only workers. The owner-workers have guaranteed jobs for life, fully adequate take-home incomes, nearly equal participation in their firms' profits and losses, equal shares in the democratic control of their enterprises, and broad and adequate health insurance, unemployment, and pension programs. Worker productivity is among the highest in Europe.

Mondragon is self-consciously based on a different picture of reality than either capitalism or socialism. It is a picture that embodies concepts of wholeness, unity, cooperation, win-win thinking, and familial relationships. People choose to produce high quality products and services because they enjoy doing so in a familial grouping, and because they see it as a service to humanity rather than primarily for personal profit. Interestingly enough, the Mondragon achievement is close to the "cooperative commonwealth" that was the aim of rural America in the nineteenth century, before the dream was eroded by the urban migrations. The basic concept of cooperative enterprise has a long history in Europe as well. The pattern seems likely to play an important role in the future because it is so in tune with the emerging values.

We can anticipate a diversity of organizational forms to be experimented with as society moves through this transition period; it is unlikely that many will copy exactly the Mondragon pattern. But two features of this model—the central emphasis on *relationships*, and ownership and management participation by employees—will no doubt be repeated with great frequency.

Promon International, Brazil, is a professional services organization active in engineering, geophysics, and electronics. It is totally owned by its 3,000 employees. Nobody can own more than 5 percent of the capital and the shares are not transferrable; in the event of death, retirement, or termination of employment, they are repurchased by the company. However, as the Chairman, Tamas Makray, contends, participation in the capital of the company would be meaningless unless it were accompanied by participation in the life of the organization—"in a creative, living, dynamic community. The purpose of Promon is to create conditions for professional and personal fulfillment and realization."

The New Goals of Business

Twenty years ago the Rouse Company was almost unique in the goals it professed and practiced. Basically, they turned the usual goals statement on its head. The first goal was to be a place in which people came together to do work that was fulfilling, and that promoted their own personal and professional development. The second goal was to conduct activities the product of which would be useful and meaningful to society—in this case, through land development. (The Rouse Company was the developer responsible for the model city of Columbia, Maryland.) The third goal was to achieve the first two so well that profit would automatically follow. People first; profit definitely in the picture, but mainly as a control signal.

These goals of the Rouse Company, almost unheard of two decades ago, are as good a model as one could find of the goals of business in a learning society.

Industrias Villares SA, a family-owned Brazilian corporation in the field of steel production and processing, is one example of a company serious about the centrality of employees' personal development. The firm's educational Institute, which places strong emphasis on helping individuals remove blocks to intuition and creativity, is available to all 20,000 employees. Vice Chairman Luiz D. Villares views enterprise as the dominant institution in the present world transformation, and sees within the enterprise a transition which "is taking us from specific roles and distinct positions to a shared responsibility; from a competitive, hierarchically dependent behavior to an interdependent, cooperative attitude; from considering work as a mean, by which some earn their living and others accumulate wealth, to envisioning work as an instrument for self-realization and personal growth; from managing workers as resources to dealing with them as beings in constant evolution and co-creators of well-being and wealth; from tradition and experimentation as the leading guides of entrepreneurial behavior to vision as the main influence on entrepreneurial decision-making and action." (Quoted in Mario Kamenetzky, "Attitudes and Perceptions in Management Practices," unpublished manuscript.)

The New Leadership

Max De Pree, chairman and former CEO of Herman Miller, Inc., is one of America's most admired industrial leaders. In his recent book *Leadership is an Art*, he lists the characteristics of a "future leader." First on his list is "has consistent and dependable integrity." Integrity has always been important; because of the changes in values and motivations of those led, it is now crucial.

But leadership is not just a function of the person "on top." Taking the systemic view, and considering the tasks that will be of concern, it is clear that leadership can be contributed from anywhere in the system.

For example, Semco, a Brazilian medium-technology manufacturing company, embodies a rather extreme form of self-management and distributed responsibility. It is based on three values: democracy, profit sharing, and information. The company's 800 employees are treated, as President Ricardo Semler puts it, "like responsible adults"; they are put in the demanding position of using their own judgment and sense of responsibility. There are no time clocks; employees come and go according to their own schedules. There are no company dress codes, no company rules about travel expenses, no security searches or store-room padlocks. Managers are evaluated by their subordinates. Important decisions are made with company-wide participation. Employees have complete access to the company's vital statistics—costs, overhead, sales, payroll taxes, profits.

Perry Pascarella, executive editor of *Industry Week*, saw the new climate coming some years ago. In a book entitled *The New Achievers* (1984) he wrote:

> A quiet revolution is taking place ... in the business corporation.... Although we have been hearing more and more about corporate efforts in human resource development in recent years, we may miss the essential truth about what is happening:

Individuals are awakening to the possibility of personal growth and finding opportunities to attain it. The team building we hear about is secondary to the development of the individual.... Management is heading toward a new state of mind—a new perception of its own role and that of the organization. It is slowly moving from seeking power to empowering others, from controlling people to enabling them to be creative.... As managers make a fundamental shift in values ... the corporation [undergoes] a radical reorientation to a greater worldview.

The economic activities of the world business system have been a major contributing factor to the global problems the whole world now faces. But by the same token, world business can be a key factor in their ultimate resolution. But not without a near-total transformation of what business is about.

Business crosses national boundaries with much more ease than do political institutions. The business corporation is a far more flexible and adaptive organization than the bureaucratic structures of governments and international public-sector institutions. Leaders in business are the first true planetary citizens: They have worldwide capability and responsibility, and their domains transcend country frontiers. Their decisions affect not just economies, but societies; not just the direct concerns of business, but world problems of poverty, environment, and security.

However, up to now this vast planet-wide business system has been subject to no adequate guiding ethic. Although these executives and their organizations comprise a worldwide economic network, there has been within that network no tradition of, and no institutionalization of, a philosophy capable of wisely guiding its shaping force. The legitimacy of business under such conditions has been called into question.

Challenges to the Individual and the Organization

Inherent in this picture of a society transforming itself are severe challenges to the individual; since we all face them, we can draw strength from one another. One is developing the willingness to change, to grow, to let go of the familiar and the well tested—in order to be able to traverse this transition period without undue stress. Another challenge is developing an inner sense of security, for there will be times when the outer environment is anything but stable and dependable. Individual-group-humanity are all involved in the action; paradoxically, we have to take responsibility for our own lives and also recognize the need for the support and guidance of others. "Think globally, act locally" says something of the same thing; we have to act where we are, but in the light of a vision of the whole.

The transition involves a widespread and fundamental change of mind—a *metanoia*. Looking forward, the task looks impossibly difficult because the change of mind has not yet taken place and we have no instruction manual on how to bring it about. Looking backward, the transition will no doubt look simple, and we will be wondering why we didn't get around to it sooner.

Perhaps a couple of diagrams will help. Individuals and organizations are undergoing change. We can summarize much of what has been said about this by focusing on (a) levels of perception in the individual, and (b) stages in evolution of the organization.

Levels of individual perception. Individuals as well as organizations evolve. At the core of this evolution is some set of assumptions or basic beliefs, about the nature of self, others, and the universe. These internalized basic assumptions, almost entirely at an unconscious level, shape the way the environment is perceived. But perceptions, in turn, have some effect on the internalized beliefs.

Many individuals today are going through a change in perception which we have tried to indicate as level 4 in the accompanying table. Why is this happening? There is no generally agreed upon answer to that question, just as there is no answer for a similar question about the societal changes described in Chapter 3. Nevertheless, as individuals change in large numbers, it is bringing about changes in organizations. These can be partly understood in terms of shifting levels of perception. These levels or modes of perception affect the quality of life of the individual; collectively, they affect how an organization or a society deals with the problems it faces.

Persons whose internalized beliefs and values place them at level 1 tend to feel they have no choice of action; no capability to determine their own lives. They feel victims of their environment. They are reactive, and have relinquished integrity and responsibility for their own being. They cling to preconceptions of security; they settle for survival. If life were a movie, such a person would be playing a bit part in his own life.

Perhaps the majority of persons in industrialized society come in at level 2 (on the chart on the following page). They tend to perceive

Four Levels of Perception

	Mode of Perception	Characteristics	Lifestyle	Key Relationships
4	Discriminating awareness	Integrity, wisdom compassion	Spontaneously creative, at home in own body and on planet	Supra-personal
3	Intuition	Self-acceptance, insight	More using full potential and spiritual possibilities	Trans-personal
2	Intellect reason	Intention	Conditioned, time-driven, need to control, competitive	Personal
1	Instinct	Security, survival	Reactive, self as victim, integrity relinquished	Sub-personal

their environment, and possible strategies for dealing with it, through a relatively fixed set of values and beliefs. They allow themselves to be conditioned by society to be one-track thinkers, time-driven, responsive to environment, and striving for perfection. The environment is perceived as a resource, to be exploited, treated as a commodity, turned into possessions and profit. Emotions are rationalized. Dualities play a commanding role in such a person's life; they seem to oppose each other (good-bad, masculine-feminine, reason-intuition), resulting in competitiveness and need for control. This person is playing the main role in the movie of his/her life.

The person who opens perception sufficiently to completely accept him/herself and admit the full spectrum of intellectual, emotional, and spiritual possibilities is depicted in level 3. This person makes great use of intuition to enhance learned knowledge and the rational mind. Judgmental thinking is replaced by a discriminating mind, allowing for the acceptance of ambiguity and the appreciation of diversity, and reducing the need for control. This lets in more of the variety of reality, permitting a wider range of experiences and allowing comfort with uncertainty. Dualities seem no longer to require either-or decisions; they complement one another, allowing for a wider range of opportunities and more choice. There is less need to alter the environment to fit internalized concepts of what should be; the concepts can be changed instead. It is comfortable to take an ecological view of the total environment. Such a person plays a starring role in his/her life, and directs the movie as well.

Level 4 is meant to indicate that rare person who has integrated body, emotions, mind, and spirit into a whole, unified organism, which resonates and harmonizes with the environment, enabling spontaneous creative response, high-level performance, and feeling completely at home in one's body and on this planet. Such a person is star, director, and scriptwriter of his/her life.

In terms of these levels of perception, the present transformation of large numbers of persons in industrialized societies can be conceived as a shift from level 2 to level 3, with an increasing number rising to level 4. Organizations are shifting from encouraging level 2 perception to fostering level 3. More importantly, the underlying collective belief system is shifting to recognize the possibility and validity of level 4 perception. These changes are congenial to more employee participation and identification with the enterprise; more flexibility and creativity; higher trust and more integrity; better symmetry among shareholders, managers, employees, customers, and community. They will contribute to economy becoming an organic part of ecology, hence to the resolution of the most vexing global problems. There is a critical need to go beyond conventional solutions. The shift described above will make that more likely.

Stages of organizational evolution. The diagram on the next page suggests the kind of evolutionary development that is taking place in corporations and other organizations as they are encountering, internally and externally, more and more persons perceiving at levels 3 and 4.

The Evolution of Organizations*

	1. REACTIVE	2. RESPONSIVE	3. PROACTIVE	4. "NEW PARADIGM"
TIME FRAME	Past	Present	Future	Flow
FOCUS	Diffused focus	Output focused	Results focused	Quality; growth of people
PLANNING	Justification; little planning	Plan for anticipated situation	Strategic planning	Intuition-guided evolution
CHANGE MODE	Punitive	Adaptive	Planned	Programmed
MANAGEMENT	Top-down decisions; fix blame	Manage through coordination	Manage through alignment	Provide vision and leadership
STRUCTURE	Fragmented	Hierarchical	Matrix organization	Self-directed networks
INDIVIDUAL'S PERSPECTIVE	Self-centered; personal	Team performance	Organization effectiveness	Culture, nation, world
ASSUMED MOTIVATION	Avoid pain; immediate rewards	Economic and status rewards	Contribution and recognition	Personal self-actualization
DEVELOPMENT THROUGH	Continued survival	Cohesion	Attunement to well-being of the whole	Continued transformation
COMMUNICATION	Orders and incentives from top down	From the top, informed by feedback	Communication both up and down	Empathic communication throughout
LEADERSHIP	Enforcing	Coaching	Purposing	Empowering

*Adapted from High Performance Programming: A Framework for Transforming Organizations by Tyler (Linda) Nelson and Frank Burns, in John D. Adams (1984).

Perhaps in trans-modern society it will really be true that corporations and other organizations are essentially arenas of interaction where people come together to learn how to care, to work together, to allow their creativity to flourish, to find meaning, and to love.

Summary

The industrialized world is going through a profound change which involves reassessment of the most basic assumptions underlying Western society, its technological infrastructure and the world economy. Among the most fundamental aspects of this transition is the role of work, in the individual's life and in society.

We typically overlook a fundamental dilemma regarding work in modern society. On the one hand, it is assumed that the destiny of practically every individual is to have a job in the mainstream economy (or at least to be married to someone who has a job, or to be in training for a job). On the other hand, work has been implicitly defined as something to be avoided, by turning it over, in increasing amounts, to automated machines. Thus, since labor productivity is continually increasing, if everyone is to have a job, *the economic product must increase more rapidly than the growth of the workforce.* The net result is tremendous pressure toward growth of economic product—through increased consumption, world militarization, and hidden makework. That pressure is now encountering counter-pressure from environmental damage and other planetary limitations. Thus an inescapable dilemma looms: There seems no way to avoid a worsening tradeoff between unemployment and further environmental deterioration and other negative consequences of over-consumption.

The work dilemma is but one aspect of a multifaceted situation which can only find satisfactory resolution through a fundamental whole-system change. A scenario involving *such change is plausible because of three converging factors.*

Factor one is the growing number and proportion of problems—global environmental deterioration; the possibility of irreversible man-made climate change; the extinction at an alarming rate of more and more species of plants and animals; deforestation and desertification; scarcity of fresh water; accumulations of toxic chemicals; chronic poverty and hunger in large portions of the world; the persistent social problems of crime, terrorism, and drug addiction; instability of the debt-ridden world economy; and, of course, the ever-present threat of international conflict with use of nuclear weapons. The list seems to be endless, and all of the problems are interrelated so that measures taken to ameliorate any one of them sends reverberations throughout the whole system.

A diversity of social and political movements comprise a second part of the picture—movements promoting democracy, liberation, ecological awareness, feminine consciousness, world peace, and social justice.

Thirdly, at a deeper level in the structure of society we can find indications of a revolutionary shift in the most basic assumptions about the nature of reality—assumptions that underlie modern society and all its institutions. It is a shift away from the materialism inherent in reductionistic science, and toward a recognition that our picture of reality is incomplete and misleading so long as it does not explicitly recognize the extent and magnificence of the potentialities of the human spirit.

The primary investigators in this project have been watching these highly interconnected developments for some years and have been struck by the fact that reassessing the role of work, which seems so central to the ultimate resolution of our dilemmas, is so little talked about. The possibility that the world economy will not be able in the future to provide anything like full employment, as that term has been conventionally understood, is such a threatening idea that the topic almost seems to be taboo. Reports that many workers in the modern economy are alienated and find their work meaningless are also threatening in their implications. Furthermore, those who discuss the economics of work seldom deal adequately with issues of meaning, and those who are concerned with the ways people seek to discover the meaning of life seldom appear competent to deal with the economics of work.

If there has been a reluctance to face certain aspects of the work issue, it is no doubt partly because the problems appear to be so intractable. And indeed they are, if one assumes that they must somehow be solved through actions of governments or top-down management. So many things have been tried—from job-creation and vocational education programs to more thoroughgoing changes such as the welfare state and centrally planned communist state—and there have been so many disappointments!

Yet there is another possibility, which, when it is viewed in the light of recent developments in Eastern Europe, China, and other parts of the world, seems far more plausible than would have been the case a decade ago. There is the possibility that the dilemmas are resolvable through a still more fundamental transformation of modern industrial society—a transformation which could come about, not through clever management from a powerful state or transnational institution, but through a bubbling up of new goals, values, commitments, and concepts, coming from a vast "creative middle band" of people who sense a new vision and will be content with nothing less than its actualization.

Somewhat as the people of Eastern Europe, in the latter part of the 1980s, awakened to their power to bring about increased liberty and democracy, so it may be—and our research would so suggest—that another awakening is underway in the Western countries. This is an awakening to the power to bring about a society in which such concepts as unemployment and "meaningless" labor are obsolete, a society in which everyone has the opportunity to be engaged in dignified and satisfying work. This awakening is not being led by some charismatic leaders, political or otherwise; rather, it is arising in what appears to be a spontaneous manner, out of the deeper values and intuition of tens of millions of people. It might be interpreted as evidence that modern society is in the process of healing itself.

Whereas there is undoubtedly a great deal of denial with regard to recognizing the true depth and seriousness of present societal and global problems, there appear at the same time many indications of spontaneous creative response. These include the social movements already referred to, as well as a host of innovative experiments in nonprofit organizations, intentional communities, alternative economies, alternative health-care programs, new forms of business entrepreneurship, citizen approaches to assisting new enterprise and community development in Third World countries, and many others.

In this report we explore the optimistic hypothesis that much of what we see going on around us can be interpreted as self-healing impulses, partially unconsciously guided. We make a case that the movements for personal and social transformation which have developed spontaneously over the last 30 years contain within them the elements of successful resolution of our most vexing dilemmas.

This is all of the greatest significance to business in particular. In the first place, making good corporate decisions depends critically on accurate assessment of both the external and the internal environment. But also, and most importantly, business leadership is in a unique position from which to contribute constructively to this peaceful transformation.

Business in Transformation

by Stanford M. Janger and Amy C. Edmondson

The CEO was certain about the acquisition of the company. The numbers were right, the product was right, the price was right. After making his recommendation to buy, he presented the package to his employees for a vote. Strong arguments were presented. Ballots were distributed throughout the company.

The employees voted it down. They weren't majority stockholders—far from it—but this was a company that believed in "democracy in action." The CEO later explained that this was "a company that I'm still sure we should have bought. But they felt we weren't ready to digest it, and I lost the vote. In a case like that, the credibility of our management system is at stake. Employee involvement must be real, even when it makes management uneasy. Anyway, what is the future of an acquisition if the people who have to operate it don't believe it's workable?"[1]

What's going on here? At a time when the media brings us ominous tales of exotic corporate raiders, leverage buyouts, "cashing out" business operations, mass layoffs, and short-term management objectives, is the above scenario a fantasy—some kind of vision of a workplace utopia? Or is this, instead, a living example of a new paradigm, a precursor of the way companies will actually "do business" as we move towards the third millennium?

Managing Without Managers

The above scenario actually took place at Semco, a Brazilian manufacturing company that is a truly remarkable illustration of the new phrase "corporate transformation." What can we learn from this apparently idyllic working environment? Let's look more closely at the way this company "does business" today. Semco "treats its 800 employees like responsible adults," according to company President Ricardo Semler. "Most of them—including factory workers—set their own working hours. All have access to the company books. The vast majority vote on many important corporate decisions. Everyone gets paid by the month, regardless of job description, and more than 150 of our management people set their own salaries and bonuses."[2]

Semco's five factories produce a range of products, including digital scanners, marine pumps, commercial dishwashers, truck filters, and mixing equipment. The company has a unique concept of management—not only for Brazil—but even when compared to the most progressive American or European companies. Semco's management is based around three fundamental values: democracy, profit sharing, and information.

Workplace Democracy

Democracy, or employee involvement, involves creating an atmosphere where workers care about productivity and company profits. Semco has discovered that the most effective production unit consists of about 150 people. (Interestingly, Bill Gore, of W.L. Gore & Associates, identified the same ideal group size described below. Is there something special about the dynamics of an aligned 150-person group?) To enable workplace democracy, Semler believes, requires the size of productive units to be small enough to put employees in touch with one another so they can coordinate their work.

There are three management layers and four titles in the company. Employees often make higher salaries than their supervisors. People are not hired or promoted until they've been interviewed and accepted by all their future subordinates. Managers are evaluated twice a year by their subordinates. Twice a year every employee anonymously fills out a questionnaire about top management competence and company credibility. It includes such questions as what it would take to make them quit or go on strike.

Important decisions are often made by company-wide vote, as depicted above, and this has tested the company's commitment to participatory management. In another instance, in selecting a plant location for Semco's marine division, employees located a building and outvoted management, so the company bought the building and moved in. The layout for a flexible manufacturing system was designed by the workers, and they hired one of Brazil's top artists to paint the whole building including the machinery. Semler says, "That plant really belongs to its employees. I feel like a guest every time I walk in."[3]

Company credibility and the democracy concept is an ongoing process, according to Semler. The underlying axiom of Semco's management philosophy is to give employees control over their own lives. The company has abolished norms, manuals, rules, and regulations. "Common sense" has replaced the rule book. "Common sense," says Semler, "is a riskier tactic because it requires personal responsibility." It also requires "just a touch of civil disobedience every time someone calls attention to something that's not working." In short, "we had to free the Thoreaus and the Tom Paines in the factory and come to terms with the fact that civil disobedience was not an early sign of revolution but a clear indication of common sense at work." Employees are put in the demanding position of using their own judgment. There are no company dress codes, no company rules about travel expenses, no security searches or store-room padlocks.

Adults at Home and at Work

"In a word," says Semler, "we hire adults, and then we treat them like adults. Think about that. Outside the factory, workers are men and women who elect government, serve in the army, lead community projects, raise and educate families, and make decisions every day about the future. Friends solicit their advice. Salespeople court them. Children and grandchildren look up to them for their wisdom and experience. But the moment they walk into the factory, the company transforms them into adolescents. They have to wear badges and name tags, arrive at a certain time, stand in line to punch the clock or eat their lunch, get permission to go to the bathroom, give lengthy explanations every time they're five minutes late, and follow instruction without asking a lot of questions."[4]

Semco has also eliminated time clocks—putting the concept of trust into action. Employees come and go according to their own schedules—even on the factory floor. The company's cellular manufacturing system makes this possible. Each "cell" makes a product—a scale, a slicer, a mixer, etc. Each cell is self-contained, so products and problems are segregated. Workers in each cell set their schedules and monthly product quotas. Several years ago, when they introduced flexible hours, it was decided to hold regular follow-up meetings to track problems and deal with abuses and production interruptions. So far they haven't held the first meeting.

Semco has a liberal profit-sharing plan supported by the way information is shared in the company. Both are discussed below.

In order for this process to work, Semler says, the company is rigorous about the numbers.

> We want them in on the fourth day of the month so we can get them back out on the fifth. And because we're so strict with the financial controls, we can be extremely lax about everything else. Employees can paint the walls any color they like. They can come to work whenever they decide. They can wear whatever clothing makes them comfortable. They can do whatever the hell they want. It's up to them to see the connection between productivity and profit and to act on it.
>
> *And that's all there is to it. Participation gives people control of their work, profit sharing gives them a reason to do it better, information tells them what's working and what isn't.*[5]

Corporate Transformation Realized

What Semler has described above can rightly be considered a worker's paradise, a truly humane way to run a company. If we are to believe Semler and a host of other advocates of corporate transformation, it's also a great way to make a company prosper. Semco was close to financial disaster in 1980, before it embarked on an ambitious transformation program. It is now one of Brazil's fastest growing companies, with a profit margin in 1988 of 10 percent on sales of $37 million. Doing good is apparently profitable.

One recent indication of the extent of change taking place is that respected management publisher Jossey-Bass released a book entitled *Corporate Transformation*, a collection of papers by consultants, academics, and business executives across the United States. To compile this volume, a call for papers was sent to thousands of professional societies and corporations, and a panel of experts made the final selection. The contributions are based on years of executive and consulting experience with organizational change. According to editors Ralph Kilmann and Teresa Covin, "Corporate transformation is a new phenomenon. Never before in the history of the world have so many organizations had to question their very purpose, strategy, structure, and culture as they have had to do in the 1980s. No senior executives of any organization today could or would dispute that one of their major responsibilities is to revitalize their organizations for a competitive world."[6]

Transformational change describes change occurring throughout an organization that is both comprehensive in scope and fundamental in nature. "Corporate transformation is a process by which organizations examine what they were, what they are, what they will need to be, and how to make the necessary changes. Implementing those changes affects both psychological and strategic aspects of an organization. The term corporate is used to convey the comprehensive effort required, in contrast to a piecemeal or single-division effort. Transformation indicates the fundamental nature of the change, in contrast to a mere linear extrapolation from the past. Corporate transformation is serious, large-scale change that demands new ways of perceiving, thinking, and behaving by all members of the organization."[7]

Transformation—The Critical Elements

If there is a revolution underway in business, just what constitutes this "transformation"? After an extensive review of current business literature along with interviews with some of America's leading management consultants, a fair amount of consensus exists about the critical elements of corporate transformation.

Primary among these elements is a strong sense of purpose. Work must be meaningful; people must feel that they are contributing in some way to individual lives and to society. Secondly, an air of openness pervades these companies; people feel free to speak up and feel confident that they will be told about critical information that affects their jobs and lives. Thirdly, a strong current of fair and democratic compensation practices is in evidence in all the readily available examples of companies in transformation. Similarly, the phrase "people are our most important resource" is not just an empty slogan. Transforming companies genuinely value their people, and as a result the trust and respect goes both ways. And finally, an unquenchable thirst for excellence characterizes these organizations; their people are energetic and ambitious. They strive to be the best in their industries.

In the pages below, we will introduce some of the people studying this phenomenon, look at the concept of corporate transformation and examine each of these five characteristics in more detail. Then, we will look at four areas where there is some disagreement in the field. Consultants and authors disagree as to whether these companies must be relatively small in size or whether transformation can occur in the Fortune 100. Secondly, there is a lack of consensus as to whether personal transformation at a broad scale is a necessary prerequisite to organizational transformation. There is also some question about the role of "corporate culture" in transformation. Lastly, there is some uncertainty about the process of transformation—does it have to be top-down (directed by the CEO or upper management), bottom-up (from middle management or even workers on the factory floor), or some organic mixture of the two?

Purposeful Work

The quest for meaning and purpose is becoming a central focus for many as the twentieth century draws to a close. A client says to a consultant, "I have realized that the way I spend my working day turns out, in time, to be the way I spend my life."[8] The workplace has become the central institution of society, largely replacing the family, the place of worship, and the community. The company (or employer) is often in the best position to become the "source of inspiration and purpose" in the life of the working-person. It is becoming more important for organizations to come to terms with this inherent need of the modern worker. This focus on purpose was seen as the most significant guidepost separating the "potentially great" companies from the traditional or old guard by most of those interviewed in this study.

Increasingly, many are finding that it is no longer enough to "have a job" or even a "career." Such people are looking for deeper meaning in their lives. Past measures of success such as material gain, status, or position no longer satisfy a fulfillment need that many are experiencing. These people are increasingly concerned about what consultant Sabina Spencer refers to as a "deeper sense of life purpose." She explains,

> They talk of making a difference, of creating meaningful work, of being fully alive, of living with integrity, of developing sacredness in their relationships, and of turning the organizational environment into a community where everyone can 'learn and grow.'... Meeting bottom line objectives and making sure the

'numbers' are right is not enough. We are seeing greater attention focused on personal and organizational vision, quality of life, personal empowerment, a sense of organizational community, and an increasing desire to influence the future health and well-being of our home planet Earth.[9]

Making Life Whole

The need to seek out purpose is felt in personal lives as well as in work lives. The need for purpose is a powerful force for bringing these two often separate parts of our life into a seamless whole. When the purposes of the organization we work for match or echo personal purpose, we experience a greater sense of personal fulfillment.

For many, personal growth is a significant aspect of their purpose. In an article entitled "The Actualized Worker," Marsha Sinetar describes the importance of personal growth.

> A key management issue of the year 2000 will be these workers' increasing need for self-actualization. By actualization I mean a healthy personality, wholeness, a full-functioning being, and psychological 'completion.' The self-actualized person is creative, independent, and self-sufficient. These individuals will increasingly have as their primary focus personal goals, inner values, and the creation of distinct lifestyles.[10]

Sinetar elaborates as to the nature of this increasingly widespread individual quest.

> Two central values of actualization have enormous economic and cultural ramifications in the workplace of the future, and clearly these can be seen to have escalated in importance to individual workers in the past two decades. These values are social transcendence and self-transcendence. By social transcendence I mean an individual's achievement of emotional independence from societal influences, including those of authority figures, family, co-workers, and other previously significant persons. The person who has detached emotionally from a known, familiar, and comfortable way of life in order to embark upon an uncharted journey is 'socially transcendent' and usually is also on the road to actualization.

She further believes that this kind of personal journey will be an invaluable asset to future businesses.

> This, then, is the top-of-the-line worker of tomorrow: a man or woman who is confident, independent, creative. He or she seeks to merge inner truths and values with outer realities, hoping to

embody—in daily life and through a life's work—the light, ideals, and unique talent found within. These workers will not structure their lives around just any 'job,' but will strive to incorporate whatever work they do into a meaningful and fulfilling life context—one that is both inwardly rewarding and outwardly creative.[11]

This phenomenon of a focus on purpose can also be described as a search for meaning. Work can be the way people derive their life's meaning. We often define our identity by our work: "I'm a secretary." "I'm a bricklayer." "I'm a lawyer." Yet, as discussed above, merely having a job doesn't necessarily make the work meaningful. When people *don't* perceive that they can make a difference—have a positive effect on their world—they often feel that work is empty or insignificant. A fulfilled worker feels that his or her work has "meaning," and often expresses this by saying that he or she has "more than a job." This often means that they see what effect they are having on a "bigger picture." Work perhaps has the most meaning when a person feels that he is making a valuable contribution to society.[12]

Profit "On Purpose"

At Patagonia, the northern California company best known for its high quality, rugged, colorful line of outdoor clothing, profit is far from an end in itself. Profit is important because, as founder Yvon Chouinard says, "The more profit we make the more we can give away. Today the only profits we pull out of the company, 10 percent before taxes, go to environmental causes." Pre-tax profits in 1988 were about $6.5 million from revenues of $76 million. Several years ago Chouinard planned to sell the company, reflecting later, "I'd never before equated business with doing anything good." He decided to stay in order to guide the company toward becoming a positive force in solving environmental problems. Patagonia gives money to about 250 organizations. It has a goal of recycling 70 percent of all the waste produced by the company as well as in the homes of employees, and is working to get other companies involved in this effort. Chouinard believes that the company attracts employees "who wouldn't have come to work for us if we didn't give money away. Our CEO came from the Yosemite Institute and wouldn't have come to Patagonia if we hadn't had this philosophy."[13]

In short, a sense of purpose is often manifested in external good deeds. For example, Fel-Pro Company, a manufacturer of engine gaskets and sealants based in Skokie, Illinois, finances a "Better Neighborhood Fund." Employees involved in community organizations can ask for donations on the group's behalf. Requests are reviewed by a committee, and Fel-Pro often makes sizable donations. "This program has given an incredible sense of pride to employees involved in charitable work," says industrial relations manager Bob O'Keefe. "And they love the fact that the company thinks enough of them to do this."[14]

Author and entrepreneur Paul Hawken sums up the role business can play in demonstrating important global values: "Business in all its manifestations offers us as rich and important a way to improve ourselves and the world around us—as does any institution. We go into business not merely to become rich, but to become who we are. We are not trying to make money, but are attempting a much more important task: to remake our world."[15]

The Body Shop—A Culture of Purpose

The Body Shop International could be the ultimate example of a company that "does well by doing good." The British company, which produces and sells cosmetics and personal care products, has grown into a $125 million-a-year enterprise with 320 outlets from the Arctic Circle to Australia. The first two American stores, in Manhattan and New Jersey, were opened in 1988. One remarkable feature of the company is that it comprises a chain of stores, mostly franchises, does not advertise, and fills its shelves with plain bottles containing soaps, scents, lotions and shampoos that don't promise beauty or youth but pledge only to "cleanse, polish, and protect the skin and hair."

Founder Anita Roddick explains, "What distinguishes us from our competitors is that we're value-led rather than market-driven. We've always worked with the same principles: no animal testing, close-to-source ingredients, no hype, no advertising and minimal packaging. In short, we respect people and the environment."[16]

Perhaps most notable is Roddick's passionate concern for environmental and community issues, and how this concern is an important part of the "culture" that permeates the Body Shop organization. All employees, from salesclerks through management, are encouraged to get involved in community projects—*on company time.* Staffs of some stores work with youth groups or AIDS sufferers; others visit cancer patients at local hospitals. Would-be franchisers (there is a waiting list of 5,000 in England alone) must demonstrate a concern for environmental issues.

The Body Shop has funded a Boys' Town and training school for destitute children in southern India and a papermaking plant in Nepal where women make scented drawer liners from banana leaves and water hyacinths. The Body Shop buys these Third World products— and pays First World prices. The organization maintains links with environmental organizations such as Greenpeace and Friends of the Earth and recently spent $1 million funding a hospital to develop artificial skin for burn victims.[17]

Along with these benevolent practices, continuous learning is an important element of the Body Shop culture. "We educate, educate all the time," says Roddick. "There's training in the shops, a training school in London, and one in New York. Not for sales. We have courses about body care, but also on topics like drugs and urban survival. For courses on aging we bring in anthropologists and elderly women. We have AIDS sufferers come in to talk. We have a video company and send out a video once a month for all staff, including franchise staff, showing community projects we're involved in. It's understood when you come in as a franchisee that you should be involved in community projects—a battered women's shelter, an AIDS program, whatever—and that your staff should participate during working hours."[18]

How "well" does the company fare by "doing good"? In 1987, when the Confederation of British Industry named the Body Shop its Company of the Year, its revenues rose by 64 percent to $53 million, pretax profits soared by 74 percent to $11 million, and Roddick received the Order of the British Empire.

The Role of Corporate Purpose

Perry Pascarella and Mark A. Frohman, in *The Purpose-Driven Organization*, discuss the importance of defining and developing a corporate purpose in order to create a framework for making decisions that will unleash a company's potential for creativity, initiative, and innovation—and allow the company to clearly and thoughtfully move into an uncertain future.[19]

In an article entitled "Strategies for a New Age," Roger Harrison writes that purpose is more important than planning in organizational change. "Purpose and intention are far more powerful than plans. Never in my years as a consultant have I seen an organization changed in any fundamental way through rational planning. The leaders I have seen deeply influence their organization's characters and destinies have always operated out of intuition, guided by strongly held purposes and drawn on by a vision of a better future. They communicated their intentions verbally to others who could share their vision, and they communicated it daily to others through their 'real time' actions and decisions. In due course, enough people shared the vision and the intention to reach 'critical mass,' and the dream became reality."[20]

In his book *Vanguard Management*, University of Southern California management professor James O'Toole writes of "Vanguard" companies where there is "commitment in word and deed to a higher purpose: These corporations exist to provide society with the goods and services it needs, to provide employment, and to create a surplus of wealth (profit) with which to improve the nation's general standard of living and quality of life. In this view, profit is the means, not the end of corporate activity."[21]

Even Walmart, a veritable symbol of consumerism, has taken a recent stand in support of the environment. A lead story in *Advertising Age* quotes Sam Walton saying that as the "Green" revolution sweeps the United States, he wants to highlight product improvements which will help prevent lasting environmental problems, and that he's convinced this can make a difference.[22]

Mistrust of Big Business runs deep in the North American culture of independence. Our literature has for decades been replete with illustrations of corrupt tycoons, from Sinclair Lewis' *Babbitt* to more recent true stories, such as David Halberstam's *Reckoning*, which depicts mediocrity and corruption at Ford. Similarly, in poll after poll taken in the 1980s, Americans, while overwhelmingly supporting the free enterprise system, have continually expressed their mistrust of American business. They have most often stated a belief that corporations operate almost exclusively for the benefit of management and stockholders. When asked whom corporations *should* serve, most Americans have expressed that business should *also* operate for the benefit of employees, customers, and society in general.

How can public mistrust be addressed by a company striving to alter the way organizations have traditionally "done business"? According to Walter Haas, CEO of Levi Strauss & Co., *"by altering the behavior which causes the mistrust."* Haas "proposes that business 'make alliances with many sectors of the public,' and 'deal ethically and openly' with employees, shareholders, customers, and not the least, the general public. The social responsibility of business requires establishing standards of excellence in all phases of operation—such as truth in advertising, quality of products, accuracy of labeling, appropriate disclosure, job content, working conditions, and upward mobility for women and minorities."[23]

Haas advocates corporations taking a public stance on important issues and causes: "A corporation must stand, steadfastly, for something worthy of the efforts of its many constituencies. A prime function of top management is to articulate with consistency and clarity a central governing idea, one that appeals to a noble or high human aspiration or purpose. In effect, great corporations must be governed by great ideas."[24]

The Open Organization

A new quality of openness permeates transforming companies. Employees feel relatively free to voice their opinions, concerns, and needs, and company planning and financial information once held sacrosanct by upper management is often freely shared throughout the organization. This quality of openness extends to an openmindedness about new ideas and new ways to do things. O'Toole points out that, "In general, the managers of the Vanguard are constantly reading and rereading, questioning, thinking, rethinking, reviewing, and revising. They are willing even to rethink their most basic assumptions; willing, in short to unlearn the things that had led to past success but are likely to be anachronistic in the future. In fact, if I were forced to pick just one characteristic that distinguishes the Vanguard from the Old Guard it would be *openness to learning*."[25]

Information Sharing

The most important manifestation of this openness is access to critical information by all employees. The liberal and extensive profit-sharing program at Semco works because the employees know exactly how the company is doing. Ricardo Semler is adamant: "Complete transparency. No hocus-pocus, no hanky-panky, no simplifications." All Semco employees attend classes to learn how to read and understand the numbers, and the course is taught by one of the employee unions. Each month, all employees get a balance sheet, a profit-and-loss analysis, and a cash-flow statement for their own division. Semler explains how open information is important throughout the company. "The three monthly reports, with their 70 line items, tell us how to run the company, tell our managers how well they know their units, and tell our employees if there's going to be a profit. Everyone works on the basis of the same information, and everyone looks forward to its appearance with what I'd call fervent curiosity."[26]

Likewise, W.L. Gore & Associates, the makers of Gore-Tex, a sophisticated fabric that revolutionized outdoor clothing and camping gear, has developed an effective and successful nonauthoritarian approach to management. The company calls itself a "lattice organization." Unlike a traditional pyramidal structure, with its hierarchical management layers, an employee at Gore may interact directly with any other employee on a one-to-one basis. In effect, there is no hierarchy or chain of command. For the most part, there are no titles. All employees are called "associates," and when hired, are told to "look around and find something to do." This encourages new employees to think inventively and works to foster an atmosphere of entrepreneurship.[27]

Motorola, headquartered in Schaumburg, Illinois, stands as a reassuring illustration that Big Business can also practice open communication. The company boasts an intricate and effective process of communication. All employees are on teams and each team has one of its members on a steering committee at the next higher level in the company. These committees permit and encourage information exchange upward, downward and laterally, and allow shop floor issues to reach highest management after going through only four levels in the chain (an extremely "flat" organizational structure for a company with 95,000 employees).

The system is buttressed by Motorola's "I Recommend" plan, where every work area in the company has a bulletin board on which employees can post questions or recommendations. These can be either signed or anonymous. Either way, the supervisor responsible for the area is required to post a reply within seventy-two hours.[28]

This openness can take the form of a "game." Jack Stack, president of Springfield Remanufacturing Corporation, in Springfield, Missouri, runs the company with a unique management system he calls the Great Game of Business. This is based upon the belief that everyone must know the numbers. The "game" at SRC wouldn't be fair if the employees didn't know the rules, and the rules are the numbers. Everyone learns the rules and plays the Game, from the engine assembler to the receptionist. Every department at SRC functions as a small business, with managers and supervisors establishing budgets after consultations with the workers in that department. They review weekly income statements and react accordingly, focusing on their annual goals. SRC employees understand income statements, cash-flow analyses, inventory controls, materials flow, and basic accounting.

Stack believes that one of his primary responsibilities is *teaching people to make money*. "When people come to work at SRC, we tell them that 70 percent of the job is disassembly or whatever and 30 percent of the job is learning. What they learn is how to make money, how to make a profit. They don't have to play the game, but they do have to learn it. We teach them about after tax profits, retained earnings, equity, cash flow, everything. We teach them how to read an income statement and a balance sheet. We say, you make the decision whether you want to work here, but these are the ground rules we play by."[29]

Before receiving this education in accounting, few employees know even the basics of retained earnings and pretax profits. Afterwards, they have an understanding of the accounting behind these figures, and this understanding contributes to the profits.[30] Each week the supervisors pass out updated income statements showing the current relation to annual goals. Quarterly bonuses are tied to those goals. "So the numbers are just flying around. The more people understand, the more they want to see the results. They want to know how well they are doing and if they are contributing. There's internal competition and peer pressure, and they get caught up in it. It's a game—the Greater Game of Business, as we call it. It's a mechanism for getting people to come into work every morning and enjoy it."[31]

Compensation—Sharing the Rewards

Transforming companies work hard to design reward systems that are both equitable and motivational. A wide variety of pay systems has been developed, usually filled with incentives for productivity and innovation. Unusual benefits are found in these companies, along with generous team or group bonuses and special compensation awards.

Progressive companies now freely experiment with creative compensation packages designed to draw in, retain, and motivate workers. Tandem Computer, Inc., for example, provides its employees a sabbatical every four years as a way to help them with self-renewal needs.[32]

At SRC, under Jack Stack's leadership, profits are shared and are related to performance. Company profits determine the size of employees' quarterly bonuses as well as the value of their stock. The company instituted an Employee Stock Ownership Plan (ESOP) as an integral part of a buyout from International Harvester. Today, four-hundred thousand of the three million shares of stock outstanding are vested in the ESOP.

During the 1970s, Motorola created a Participative Management Program, or PMP. For purposes of coordination, Motorola employees are grouped into teams of 50 to 250 workers. Each employee shares in a common bonus pool with his or her other team members. The idea is that the people in each pool are responsible for their own performance—measured by the production costs and materials use that are directly controllable by the team. When an idea proposed by anyone on the team leads to a cost reduction or to production that exceeds a target, all team members share in the gains through bonuses that can amount to 41 percent of base salary (the average varies between 8 and 12 percent).[33] According to O'Toole, GM, ITT and other large companies have steadfastly claimed that it is impossible to translate the employee motivation and participation practices of successful smaller companies into the big company arena. But Motorola, with the world's biggest employee participation plan, is showing that in this case the secrets of small business success can be captured by big business.

Since initiating PMP, Motorola claims significant productivity improvement, increased cooperation, decreased employee turnover and impressive cost reductions. It has resulted in better communication between all levels, which encourages people to work together toward common objectives.

The Olga Company: Profit Sharing in an Unlikely Industry

Headquartered in Van Nuys, California, the Olga Company produces ladies' undergarments and, in an industry historically noted for worker exploitation, is an extraordinary example of treating employees as stakeholders. "Most of Olga's California-based competitors run little better than sweatshops in which women from Asia and Latin America toil in substandard working conditions for less than minimum wages. In contrast, the Olga Company not only pays better than union wages, but workers own shares in the firm and participate in profits. Moreover, they have a high degree of security against layoffs."[34]

Profit sharing is an essential feature of Olga's management values. "The Olga plan:

- Includes every member of the company.
- Is highly intensive 25 percent of pretax profits—after a 15 percent provision for stockholders' equity—is contributed to the fund).
- Provides for both profit and ownership sharing. One fifth of every year's contribution is used to purchase Olga shares for all participants in the program.
- Includes a 'Profit Sharing Through Profit Caring' program, the objective of which is to improve profits through the ingenuity, imagination, and participation of all managers and line workers."[35]

Once again, we can go back to Semco to see exemplary compensation practices. Twice a year, Semco calculates 23 percent of after-tax profit on each division income statement and gives a check to three employees who have been elected by the workers in their division. The money is invested by these three until the division meets and decides by a simple majority vote what to do with it. The decision has usually turned out to be equal distribution, so that if a division has 150 employees, the total is divided by 150 and distributed with each worker sharing equally. In short, "The guy who sweeps the floor gets just as much as the division partner." Semler says that the company's experience "has convinced me that profit sharing has an excellent chance of working when it crowns a broad program of employee participation, when the profit-sharing criteria are so clear and simple that the least gifted employee can understand them, and perhaps most important when employees have access to the company's vital statistics—costs, overhead, sales, payroll taxes, profits."[36]

Fel-Pro focuses on employees' benefits in order to instill worker loyalty. During the 48-year life of the company, it has never had a work stoppage and receives ten applications for every opening, often from friends and family of employees (10 percent of the 1,700 workers are husband-wife teams). Along with excellent "standard" benefits, Fel-Pro provides an active profit-sharing plan (the company contributes approximately 15 percent of employee salaries); group auto insurance; a company grant of $2,200 to each child of an employee toward its annual college costs (up to a total of $8,800 over four years); a $1,000 treasury security to new babies of employees (or $1,000 toward legal expenses in adopting a child); an extra day's pay for birthdays and anniversaries with the company paid vacations and many other benefits. The company conducts monthly employee forums to give employees a chance to air gripes, express views, and make suggestions.

Fel-Pro has a day care center located adjacent to the plant which provides education and recreation to children two to five years old for a tuition of $60 per week—about one-third the actual expense. It offers an accredited, state licensed kindergarten program. The company also "does its best" to allow parents to eat lunch with their children at the facility.[37]

Valuing People

How do you fill a business with good employees? According to Paul Hawken, "the best source of new employees is a satisfied worker. Create a business that is the cat's pajamas to work in, and you will be deluged with the friends, associates, and relatives of employees who would like to work with you. They will be your best recruits."[38] James O'Toole concurs, observing that "for most Americans, being treated as an adult is preferable to the most generous paternalism," pointing to a major reason why new, more empowering human resource policies and attitudes work.[39]

According to Robert Levering, co-author of *The 100 Best Companies to Work For in America*,

> Employees at 'good workplaces' often remark that the company gives them a lot of responsibility. Those who have worked elsewhere often suggest that the biggest change they

notice is the greater level of responsibility they are given.... Responsibility implies control. The issue of control strikes at the very core of what distinguishes good workplaces.... When people report that they have responsibility and control over their work, they mean that they have some power... a role in defining their own jobs—determining priorities and deadlines, and determining actions taken by others (including supervisors and top management) without fear of retribution.[40]

An indication of the change taking place in corporate circles is the increasingly popular concept and usage of the term *stakeholders*. "The premise is that it's not only stockholders who count, but all who have a stake in a company: employees, customers, suppliers, government, the community, anyone affected by corporate actions. NCR is one corporation that has been carrying this banner high, taking out a series of full-page ads in the *Wall Street Journal* and *Business Week*, proclaiming its commitment to various stakeholder groups. And in June ['88], NCR sponsored the First International Symposium on Stakeholders, inviting corporate leaders to examine questions like this one, taken verbatim from the program: 'Can Marxist claims about the "internal contradictions of capitalism" be countered with a stakeholder approach to management?'" And similarly, "Is stakeholder goodwill a fundamental component of success?"[41]

Olga proves once again to be a superb illustration of valuing people in a notoriously unstable industry. In the ladies' garment industry, with its bust-and-boom business cycles, job security is rare. Not at Olga. Since the company's founding over forty years ago, through recession and down times, Olga has never had significant layoffs. During the worst times, when competitors were shutting down, Olga implemented temporarily shortened workweeks.

Furthermore, employees are called "associates" at Olga. The late founder Jan Erteszek stated: "The people who work for us aren't hired hands. They invest their time, their efforts, and, in some cases, their lives, much as stockholders invest capital or managers invest knowledge. All three are investors. All three, therefore, have a right to share in the wealth produced by the company."[42] When asked why he believed that every one of his "associates" had a right to share in the company's profits and ownership, Erteszek responded: "Because it is the morally right thing to do."[43]

Worker Involvement in the Management Process

Olga operates as if investors, managers, and workers are involved in a "common venture enterprise," each having reciprocal rights and obligations. At "creative meetings," workers are obligated to provide ideas for new products. "Olga's designers—many of whom are from the working-class areas of the San Fernando Valley—creatively come up with designs that match and often outpace the professional haute couture designers of New York. It seems that no matter what the competition—foreign or domestic—tries, the Olga Company keeps growing, keeps earning a healthy profit, and keeps creating jobs for underprivileged minority women."[44]

At the Body Shop, employees are encouraged to express their own creativity and initiative. Posters in the stores urge the staff to "Break the Rules" and "Think Frivolously" and bonuses are paid for innovative suggestions. Similarly, the management of Rochester Products in Coopersville, Michigan, which makes fuel injectors for GM, asks employees to help evaluate potential suppliers. When deciding who should be promoted to supervisors, the company solicits advice from workers.

In an ambitious effort to create "transformation" on a grand scale, General Motors invested five-billion dollars to create Saturn Corporation in the early 1980s. The world's largest "startup" ever, Saturn was to be run with an entirely new model of management. And, awaiting release of the first automobile in 1990, the jury is still out on the Saturn "experiment." Its goal of creating a "non-hierarchical" organization from scratch—of removing power and authority by removing bosses, of putting operational decision making in the hands of the working teams, and of creating conditions that compel shared cooperation—has not been easy to implement. After all, the executives working in this new venture have more than likely brought their old GM mindsets with them into the new structure.

The management of Springfield Remanufacturing Company demonstrated how it values people by sitting down with the employees of the company to ask a simple but compelling question: "What kind of company do we want to live and work in?"[45] Paul Hawken describes the kind of employee he looks for at his remarkably successful garden tool catalogue company: "At Smith & Hawken, the quality we are most concerned with is the person's 'heart.' Is he a good person? Does he like people and want to work with them in the office and assist them as customers? Does his work express these qualities?"[46]

In the 1950s, Motorola threw away its last time clock, putting all workers on an honor system. Around the same time, the company created an employee advisory committee that reported directly to the board of directors along with separate employee task forces to review such subjects as benefits. Motorola workers were among the first in a large U.S. corporation to gain a measure of job security: A decision by the CEO was—and still is—required to fire any worker with ten years or more service in the company.

Valuing People with Feedback Systems

Invented by Patagonia's Yvon Chouinard, the 5-15 report is so named because it requires no more then fifteen minutes to write or five minutes to read. It is submitted each Friday by most employees of the company and is extremely effective in keeping everyone in touch with management and the direction of the company.

The reports are divided into three parts. The first is a simple description of what the person did during the past week. Employees find that after describing their work week after week, they are able to describe what's going on in a clearer and more detailed way. If their reports become repetitive and boring, that may signal a problem—the job may need to be revamped or made more challenging, or the employee may need a "transfusion." The second part of the report is a blunt description of the employee's morale, and an assessment of morale in his or her department. The third part requires each employee to present one idea that will improve the company, or the department, or his or her job—one idea each week, fifty-two ideas a year.[47]

Valuing People with Democracy

James Renier, President of Honeywell—one of O'Toole's "Vanguard" companies—describes another way to value people:

> When I say Democracy of the Workplace, I don't mean voting on who will be boss, or what products will be manufactured. I simply mean the establishment of a climate and work rules that respect the dignity and ability that people are assumed to have, according to the democratic principles that Americans claim to hold sacred.... We have a history of defending these principles. We have made them work in this country. They have brought us the respect and,

in some cases, the envy of the other countries of the world. But too often, here in our own country, the ideals of democracy have stopped at the factory gate.[48]

Support Beyond The Workplace

This quality of valuing people sometimes takes the form of unusual fringe benefits. Fel-Pro, for example, owns a wooded 200-acre facility in Cary, Illinois, with lakes for fishing, an olympic-size swimming pool and picnic facilities. Employees can take up to nine guests to the facility, and can send their children to day camp there for ten dollars per week (regardless of the number of children). The company also provides psychologists and counselors, income-tax preparers, and lawyers to give employees advice free of charge. While lawyers do not represent employees, the company says that 85 percent of the employees using the service only require the lawyer's advice to resolve their problems. Fel-Pro will pay a portion of the charges for individual tutoring and diagnostic testing of employees' children with learning problems. It also pays for counselors to meet with college-bound students to help them make the right choice.

Perhaps the most important indication of its genuine valuing of employees is that Fel-Pro, despite a heavy dependence on the auto industry with its lean times and cyclical layoffs, has never had a group layoff. Instead, the company will build inventories during bad times, put employees in lesser paying jobs without decreasing their salaries, or during the leanest times, cut back to four-day work weeks.[49]

Striving for Excellence

Not the least significant reason for—and characteristic of—corporate transformation is the quest for excellence. In 1984, in writing *Vanguard Management*, James O'Toole selected his own group of the best managed *large* corporations in the U.S. He called them "vanguard" in the belief that they could serve as future models for all large, publicly held corporations. These were companies that were highly profitable *and* socially responsible. They did well by doing good. The companies he selected were Atlantic Richfield, Control Data, Dayton-Hudson, John Deere, Honeywell, Levi Strauss, Motorola, and Weyerhaeuser. Each share the drive to be the best at everything they do. These companies strive for excellence in every aspect of their business. They do not accept being second rate. While other corporations may settle for being the biggest or excelling in one area, Vanguard companies are committed to being the best—in everything.[50]

Alas, as Tom Peters discovered after writing *In Search of Excellence*, the selection of a company in a "best managed" or "excellence" list is often akin to appearing on the cover of *Sports Illustrated* before the "big game." Since all companies run into trouble from time to time, perhaps a true test of a company's greatness is how its managers behave in bad times.

O'Toole's criteria for the Vanguard are centered in the belief that corporations effect the degrees of freedom and equality we all experience and that they greatly influence our standard of living and the quality of our lives. He therefore feels that it is important to continually experiment with and implement new ways to manage organizations which will enhance social justice. His standards are rigorous. Vanguard managers stick with their values, even in hard times. They demonstrate moral courage. They resist pressures for short-term actions and will risk taking an unpopular position in order to stand behind their high purpose.

Motorola—Using Change to Promote Excellence

Motorola has probably done the best job of any large U.S. business of institutionalizing change. The company has built into its culture the things that make the high-tech companies of Silicon Valley such attractive places to work. With secure jobs plus the added advantage of being an established corporation that has proved capable of adapting to changing markets and technologies, it has been able to survive adversity with its principles intact.

Prior to 1970, Motorola was a relatively low-tech company with about a quarter of its business in consumer electronics, primarily car radios and Quasar televisions. Historically, the company turned in a steady but unspectacular growth in sales of about 15 percent per annum. In the late 1960s, CEO Robert Galvin decided that the technological future lay neither with car radios nor with color TVs. The future was with higher-technology products, such as semiconductors and microprocessors. While Intel, Texas Instruments, and other competitors appeared to have had a big technological jump on Motorola—and what appeared to be an insurmountable lead in terms of the sophistication of their engineers and scientists—Galvin decided to "bet the company" and attempt to make Motorola number one in semiconductors, as well as in two-way communications where it was already number one.[51]

Galvin laid out a 10-year plan for transforming Motorola. In this, he did something unusual for an American executive; he anticipated the need for future change even though the company was not in any imminent trouble. Galvin saw that his plan could only be realized through the active support of *all* of Motorola's employees. Management realized that to compete with the Japanese required high standards of quality, productivity, cost and inventory control, customer service, and delivery. The goal was nothing less than perfection—*zero defects*. As the plan developed, it became clear to top management that a centralized, highly directive corporate structure would not produce the kind of commitment, effort, and innovation needed to succeed. The company was thus radically decentralized, creating many new "presidents," each with a small entrepreneurial business to run as he saw fit (consistent with the thrust of the overall plan). An incentive system was created for managers including a generous bonus pool that rewarded innovation, risk taking, and superior performance.

What is an "excellent" company? How does a company achieve excellence? Tom Peters says, "Excellent firms don't believe in excellence—only in constant improvement and constant change."[52] At the Olga Company, management begins with the assumption that the purpose of the business is to provide its customers with the highest quality product it can and to provide steady and meaningful employment for employees. From that, everything else done—marketing, manufacturing, product design, motivation of employees, sharing of profits—all stem from the initial premise of the purpose of the business.[53]

At Springfield Remanufacturing Corporation, in a dramatic illustration of improvement by learning from mistakes, employees responsible for major mistakes have been flown to distant cities to rectify the problems on the spot. They learn from the experience and share their insight with fellow workers, and the customer is impressed with a service he might not have expected.[54]

Uncertainties of the Process

Although there is general agreement about the importance of purpose, valuing employees, fair and generous compensation, openness in the workplace, and the need to strive for excellence, there is less consensus about 1) the size of an organization that can undergo genuine transformation; 2) the relationship between organizational change and personal change for individual employees; 3) the role of an organization's culture in the process; and 4) just how to achieve this transformation.

The Question of Size—Is Less More?

Recently, Tom Peters described the kind of business that will thrive in the present and future world of continuous change, arguing that small companies represent the success model for the future. "Make no mistake, our economy is being transformed. Is it happening fast enough? I honestly don't know. In any case, I know that the future does not belong to the companies I grew up with, the elephants that used to rule the world and that I used to serve. These wild and woolly times call for a new species of competitor—fast, agile, thriving on change. I'll cast my lot with them."[55] Peters maintains that bigger is no longer better. The economies of scale that fueled the Industrial Revolution are now less vital than the advantages that smallness offers in terms of flexibility and responsiveness.

What kind of organization will be dominant in the economy as we move into the third millennium? Paul Hawken echoes Peters: "Since 1973, the Fortune 500 companies have lost a net of 6,000,000 jobs, passed off as part of becoming 'mean and lean,' of slimming down, restructuring, and competitiveness—terms that ring hollow to the men and women who were its victims. During this same period, however, 23,000,000 net new jobs were created in the U.S. and 98 percent of them came from businesses with 100 employees or less."[56]

David Birch, author of *Job Creation in America*, notes "...there is no such thing as an American economy, at least not in the way the term is usually employed. Rather, there are about 7 million companies, close to 90 percent of which employ fewer then 20 workers. Taken together these small companies create more jobs than the Fortune 500, grow more rapidly, run greater chances of failure, and show more adaptability."[57]

Paul Hawken continues, adding support to the argument that the possibilities for transforming large organizations are limited: "Our society and economy are changing very rapidly, particularly during these past 15 years. Once a business becomes large, it cannot turn on a dime. In fact, its virtue is that it is stable, steady, and solid. It turns like a tanker and requires all the care and caution one would give to such a task. But when the rate of social change outstrips the ability of large enterprises to adapt, you get the entrepreneurial bloom that we have been witnessing, simply because small enterprises respond more quickly to how you and I are changing. We are inventing new lives, new patterns of living together, new values, and new ideas." [58]

Similarly, some claim large organizations will never boast the vitality or excitement of a small company. David Birch for example writes, "It is the difference between organization men working from nine to five and aggressive, ambitious people who are in the shop weekends and labor at low wages for a chance at a piece of the action." [59]

Others, such as GE's Jack Welch, say it's not *size*, but *simplicity*, that matters: "For a large organization to be effective, it must be simple. For a large organization to be simple, its people must have self-confidence and intellectual self-assurance.... People always overestimate how complex business is. This isn't rocket science; we've chosen one of the world's more simple professions. Most global businesses have three or four critical competitors, and you know who they are. And there aren't that many things you can do with a business. It's not as if you're choosing among 2,000 options." [60]

Along the same lines, the late W.L. Gore believed the "lattice" system of workers efficiently interacting together works because the company never allows factories to become larger then 200 employees (150 employees at each plant is considered to be ideal—a belief expressed earlier by Ricardo Semler). Whenever that critical size is reached, another factory is built. This small size allows for a great deal of direct interaction between individual workers. Gore called this system "un-management."

Many believe that "growing" a small business is not simply the expressive actions of individual entrepreneurs; rather it is how we as a nation are growing our economy. Small businesses are formed to solve problems that cannot be solved by money alone, and they are formed to change our culture itself. [61]

Meanwhile, countless managers and consultants are working to transform some of the world's largest corporations, and many are reporting progress. Motorola, discussed above, is one highly visible example of successful organization-wide change, as are the two other winners of the United States' Malcolm Baldrige National Quality Award, Xerox and Milliken. Ford Motor Company is another frequently cited example of significant and successful change in a large organization; its Team Taurus Project marked a new era of teamwork and of product quality for the old automotive giant. O'Toole selected his "Vanguard" as harbingers of the large organization of the future—a model that confidently combines largeness and flexibility. Competing theories aside, it is safe to say that it is too soon to decide this question of size as an untold number of large organizations are in the midst of undertaking ambitious change programs.

The Role of Individuals in Organizational Change

If transforming an organization means that employees need to think, respond, or behave in fundamentally different ways, this suggests that these individuals need to undergo a radical transformation as well. The question of whether personal change is a prerequisite to organizational change is a controversial one. For many employees, being part of a changing organization may involve an experience of personal crisis. Executives who have spent years learning how to "get ahead" may be asked to change the very thinking modes that made them a success in the past. Such executives may experience difficulties—even panic—when it becomes necessary to examine the basis of their own self-esteem and sense of competence. Transforming an organization may arouse deep-seated traumas, creating confusion and personal struggles in individual employees during the change process.

Many cases of employees protesting organization-wide change programs—such as the well-publicized outrage at Pacific Bell several years ago over a mandatory training program based on the work of Gurdjieff-scholar Charles Kron—have made this a controversial topic, the complexities of which will continue to haunt such efforts in the future. The focus of the controversy is typically on feared "brainwashing" and forced acceptance of new ideas that may conflict with employees' religious beliefs. This delicate relationship between individuality and a need for organizational alignment around strategic issues will be a critical subject of further discussion in this field.

Despite these possible concerns, there are many who argue that personal change is paramount. Herman B. Maynard, Jr., an executive at E.I. du Pont de Nemours & Co. and a key figure in a "planned transformation" of the company's Wire and Cable division, believes that "there is really no such thing as organizational transformation, there is only individual transformation. And there is no prescription for change. Consultants can help facilitate the process for, perhaps, the first six months. After that, you're on your own."[62]

Professor and author Peter Vaill expresses a similar belief, "[this transformation] is going to occur at personal levels as well as organizational and institutional levels. What it will look like, it's hard to predict. I think an awful lot of important people are getting very fed up with the quality of their lives, particularly the stresses and strains they're living under—the health issues, family issues, financial issues, quality of life issues."[63]

Moreover, it can be argued that democratic work environments—such as that described by Richard Semler at Semco—require such a significant degree of accountability and responsible participation by all employees that personal change, or growth, is essential.

Whatever the ultimate tide of public opinion, there is no doubt that as "change" continues to become a more significant part of corporate life, it will be increasingly important to learn how to respond and recover from major change—both organizationally and personally. By understanding the dynamics of the change process, individuals and "employees will have more energy to focus on the growth opportunities that change offers, rather than on the resistance uncertainty often engenders."[64]

Harry Woodward and Steve Buchholz, authors of *Aftershock— Helping People Through Corporate Change*, reinforce the notion that change is here to stay. "Change is one of the foremost issues, if not the foremost business issue, of our day. Beginning roughly with the publication of Alvin Toffler's *Future Shock* in 1970, 'Change'—with a capital C—entered the corporate lexicon as a word describing a mixed blessing. On the one hand, change represented growth, opportunity, and innovation; on the other hand, threat, disorientation, and upheaval. Like it or not, change has become the norm. The relatively steady, predictable economic growth that characterized the post-World War II period has given way to rapid increases in competition, limited resources, and changes in attitude about work, male-female roles, and management."[65]

The Role of Corporate Culture

The culture of a corporation can be described as "that complex, interrelated whole of standardized, institutionalized, habitual behavior that characterizes that firm and that firm only." As James O'Toole sees it, numerous corporate change efforts during the past decade have failed "because they only deal with superficial levels of culture: They deal just with cultural artifacts (like the company logo or the style of management); or they go one level deeper and attempt to change cultural values (the norms and ideals of the organization). In contrast, the process of change at the Vanguard takes root because it operates not only at these two levels, but also at the deeper level of basic assumptions."[66]

Similarly, Herman Maynard suggests being aware of the "corporate immune system" which "tries to kill off anything it senses as foreign." Culture is a powerful force in maintaining the status quo.

Pascarella and Frohman stress the importance of focusing on the central corporate purpose to positively affect the organization's culture. "Some corporate cultures have been changed unintentionally as new techniques were adopted. Despite the lack of consensus about the nature of corporate culture, some executives are trying to deliberately alter it by wrestling with such concepts as teamwork, values, vision, and mission." The authors believe, however, that, "There is little point in building teamwork ... unless the team knows what it is working toward—where the total organization is going. Mission statements also are of little value in the absence of a fully conceived management program that supports the corporate mission in every aspect of corporate activity and wins commitment."[67]

In short, culture is a powerful, but elusive, force in implementing transformational change. The role of culture in influencing behavior cannot be ignored, and yet it is unclear whether culture change is the cause or the effect of some of the other widespread changes described in this report.

The Process of Transformation—How Does It Work?

A variety of transformation models, strategies, and principles have been developed and written about by managers, consultants and professors. Author James O'Toole lists five "principles of excellence" of Vanguard Companies: stakeholder symmetry, dedication to high purpose, continuous learning, high aim and moral courage. Peter Senge, of MIT's Sloan School of Management, advocates a "new management style" to support the implementation of four critical elements—autonomous (and relatively small) business units, few levels of management, profit sharing and employee ownership, governance structures such as corporate partnerships and internal boards. Consultant Bill Veltrop focuses on four "technologies" of transformation: learning how to learn, creating shared visions, organization design, and planning and leading. Rosabeth Kanter, of Harvard Business School, emphasizes a "sociological approach," entailing "parallel structures" of entrepreneurial teams and "skunk works." Consultant Roger Harrison speaks of "attunement" and "love." Many argue in favor of "bottom-up" transformation, others "top-down," and others still, simultaneous top-down and bottom-up change efforts.

There is general agreement that a completely transformed organization does not (yet) exist. Our information about large scale, organization-wide corporate transformation is rapidly evolving. Editors Kilmann and Covin introduce their impressive volume with the following caveat: "The frontiers of knowledge in this field are pushed forward every time some significant and qualitatively different form of organization is revitalized. This state of affairs also means that organizations requiring transformation cannot wait until the knowledge base is firm and predictable. Such questions as 'can you prove to me that this process will work?' cannot be answered in the affirmative."[68]

Businesses of all sizes and products around the world are experimenting on themselves, hiring consultants, appointing "improvement practitioners" and passing out books on new management concepts, culture change and quality. The field is flooded with recommendations from such thinkers as Crosby (14 steps), Deming (14 steps) and Feigenbaum (40 steps!)[69] "Actually, any organization that plans to wait for the methods for transformation to be proven effective is probably writing its own epitaph."[70]

One of the difficulties in "mandating" a fundamental change throughout an organization has been management's inability to see just how extensive the process needs to be. Corporate leaders may be familiar with the vocabulary of change and may take an "out-front" position—even committing a major capital investment. However, that may be the extent of their commitment, not because they were unwilling to commit more but because they assume that is what their commitment needs to be.[71]

One of the major areas of disagreement about the transformational process concerns whether or not this kind of fundamental change can be "mandated" from top management. A widely voiced concern has been that top management focuses on the transformation of "them"—outside the executive suite—rather then looking at changing themselves.

O'Toole maintains that a certain degree of decentralization, or widespread participation, is essential to change. "While the mechanisms by which changes were achieved at the Vanguard vary in detail, all entailed one form or another of decentralization of decision making, monitoring of stakeholder needs, challenging of assumptions—and the provision of appropriate rewards and incentives for all of these activities."[72]

Author and consultant Harrison Owen expresses a similar belief: "My bet is that breakthroughs are going to come not because some guy at the top was really bright. I'm not excluding him, but given the amount of freedom that he or she actually has … it is minimal compared to what's happening in the rest of the organization. So I look for innovative breakthroughs not at the top, but rather at those other parts of the organization where the rubber meets the road and the right people are thinking about the wrong ideas at the opportune time. The issue then becomes—has the person at the top created an environment in which that kind of experimentation is allowed?"[73]

If "top-down" mandated change is an effective strategy for organizational transformation, then it will be worthwhile to watch General Electric—a corporation not especially noted for a tradition of "high purpose" and "stakeholder symmetry"—during the next few years. Chairman and CEO John F. Welch, Jr. has embarked on a impressive challenge: "building a revitalized 'human engine' to animate GE's formidable 'business engine.'" Welch recently stated: "Ten years from now, we want magazines to write about GE as a place where people have the freedom to be creative, a place that brings out the best in everybody. An open, fair place where people have a sense that what they do matters, and where that sense of accomplishment is rewarded in both the pocketbook and the soul."[74]

DuPont's Herman Maynard discusses some of the "softer" areas of the transformation process. He mentions "alignment of purpose, respect for the individual, steadfastness, coaching, relationships, participative processes, stress management and patience" among other elements as critical to transformation. He also asks for "continued support for personal growth" along with the "involvement of spouse and families" and "support from the community." Finally, he advocates a "trust in and use of intuition" to complement business skill. His conclusions, based on first-hand experience, represent a significant departure from our traditional concept of an engineering culture!

Change—Not If But When and How

Rapid and radical change, throughout the economy, in large organizations and small, is fast becoming commonplace. "For the first book, we had a very difficult time finding 100 good companies," says Robert Levering, co-author of the *100 Best Companies to Work for in America*, a 1984 classic on enlightened workplaces. For the next edition in 1991, "There are so many, we will probably have to eliminate good candidates."[75] It is no longer a question of whether or not companies will change, the question is how and when will they change. In a decade begun by events in Eastern Europe that outpace human imagination, will management embrace the idea that corporate transformation is a constant state—a new way of managing—and not simply a program to "tune up" the organization or a necessary one-time evil? Moreover, will controversial questions—such as whether organizations have a role in "transforming" employees—thwart the undeniable progress many businesses have made over the past few years toward creating fulfilling and empowering work environments? There is no doubt that observers of corporate transformation will continue to be fascinated by the forces supporting and inhibiting fundamental change.

Certainly there is much to instill a sense of optimism; open discussions of a "deeper sense of life purpose" in business are new and noteworthy. And yet all of this cannot be heralded without a healthy skepticism. As James O'Toole cautions us, there are those waiting quietly in the wings for their chance at retrenchment. "At each of the Vanguard there are those who are opposed to the principles of New Management and who use every downturn in profits, stock price, or the economy as an opportunity to lobby for a return to the 'tougher-minded' practices of the Old Guard."[76]

It is too soon to come to any final conclusions. And yet, if we are to see significant positive change in the uneasy state of our troubled world, it may be that business is best poised to trigger and lead that change. The situation can probably best be described as a race—against time, against the terrifying destruction of our fragile environment, against the disintegration of much of our educational system, and against increases in violence and social turbulence evident in nations around the world. What corporate transformation represents at the most basic level is the best intentions and actions of individuals and of companies toward creating a better world. The ongoing question then is, will they succeed? It is a race with an uncertain outcome, and yet, what choice do we have but to proceed?

Addendum:

As a final contribution, we would like to allow some of the writers, consultants and professors interviewed in this study to speak for themselves. Their eloquent and insightful observations are worth reading in full.

Peter Vaill, Professor of Human Systems, George Washington University, and author, *Managing as a Performing Art* (Jossey-Bass):

> There's a tremendous amount of talk, a lot of writing, a lot of enthusiastic workshops, and a fair amount of interesting experimentation going on in companies. I don't know of any company that has achieved the culture change in a company-wide sense that is implied in some of the new age visions of participatory, high quality, humanistic management environments. I personally think it's being vastly oversold. If you're talking about changing the culture of some large corporation you need to think in terms of a 10-20 year time perspective and nobody has been keeping records for that long. So while somebody in AT&T may talk about how the culture is changing, the culture of AT&T is so strong and so deep in the soul of most employees and in the surrounding culture that it's going to be a long time before it really changes.

Marsha Sinetar, educator, organizational psychologist and author, *Do What You Love, The Money Will Follow* (Dell Books):

> My term for creating options is 'creative adaptation.' In years past we adjusted to whatever were the external expectations. One went to school and lived the way one's ancestors did. There was very little demand for accommodation from the individual toward

the corporation or the external world. In other words you didn't demand that the environment bend toward you. I think what's happening now is that this is not going to work because we're losing too much talent. So the best and the brightest are somehow able to get companies to adapt to them. Some employees seem to express it better and get their way more effectively than others. You can see this phenomenon on a critical mass scale too if you look at what's happened in East Germany. The Wall coming down is a good example of collective creative adaptation. It was a coherent, peaceful accomplishment. People are just not going to submit mindlessly anymore. So institutions and organizations have to bend a bit to the ideas of the individual or the group.

Roger Harrison, consultant and author:

I see positive signs, younger managers coming along who were turned on by the visions of the 1960s and 1970s and are now getting to be in a position of power where they can dust off some of their dreams and make new things happen. So, I see two forces going on in organizations. I see the forces of hope and transformation and I also see the deadness of organizations that are constrained within and without to pay far more attention to the short-term bottom line.

Harrison Owen, consultant, author, *Spirit: Transformation and Development in Organizations* (Abbot Publishing):

My presumption is that any system is constantly adapting to its environment. By and large that adaptation and those experiments in adaptation in organizations are more likely to take place at the periphery or the side corners. Most of our organizations to this point, particularly corporations that are in any kind of product manufacturing, spend most of their time trying to control within tighter and tighter tolerances. Essentially what that does is eliminate innovation. There's reason for that. That's the way you make money—or at least that's the way you used to make money.

George Land, consultant and author, *Grow Or Die* (John Wiley & Sons):

The large mature corporations are in 'sync' with the culture at large. It was difficult for them to move ahead. Now, the larger culture is in the change phase—it has reached *breakpoint*—and you're starting to see it manifested in the corporations.

Peter Vaill:

In the U.S. and other developed countries, the nineties are going to be the *recovery* decade where we're going to start trying to think about how to recover from the 40 years of non-stop obsession with economic growth and expansion that have marked our culture.

I've referred to this as a *world of permanent white water* in which we're all roaring down a wild river, none of us feeling like we either understand or control what we're in the middle of. It's a new mentality for Americans. Americans have had the luxury of believing that they both understood and controlled the systems around them. It is obvious that neither is the case today. It's going to become more obvious to millions of people in the future so that lack of understanding and lack of control are going to be even more a fact of life 10 or 15 years from now. That has a profound impact on almost everything we do.

Marsha Sinetar:

You can't mandate motivation. You can't force people to enjoy what they're doing. You can't bring in an external person to hype up a group of people and motivate them, then leave and expect the people to stay motivated. So we realize that there's an energy exchange here. If corporations want dedication, if they want employees to invest their energy and time, they have to pay them with something more than money. Because the money exchange just doesn't work anymore. People are not slaves to the dollar and will no longer work as material slaves. This seems to be a tremendous revolution in consciousness.

Roger Harrison:

One of the most hopeful things that has happened in my lifetime is what's going on in the eastern bloc right now. There you find revolutions that are taking place without killing for the most part, except in Romania. This is certainly the most significant new departure in social change since the American and French Revolutions—which were both bloody in their own way. It's encouraging to me that change can take place in a way that involves a change of consciousness without violence on the part of the ruling class—the people in power. If that can happen in the Soviet bloc, it seems reasonable that it can happen in American organizations. You don't see it happening in these organizations much now. For the most part, people are not that disaffected, they're not pushing that hard for change. They're just kind of grumping along. Americans are very much oriented to their own personal affairs so you don't have a strong grassroots feeling that it's time to overturn the old order in organizations. So on the one hand, I see things happening in the world that suggest the possibility of massive transformation without all of the destructiveness that has usually accompanied that transformation in the past. I am not sure that large American organizations are where it's most likely to happen. At least not in the immediate future. But when it happens, it may be just as sudden as it was in Eastern Europe. The suddenness of that took everybody by such surprise that the only reasonable explanation for it would seem to be divine intervention into the hearts and minds of the people. Now that could happen in big businesses too.

Harrison Owen:

I am not at all sure that anybody is going to transform anybody. As a matter of fact I'm absolutely certain they won't. The environment of the Universe is handling that one quite well. The problem is not to introduce change. The issue is to recognize it—it's already there—and help people through it. It's not that there aren't some very powerful high human technologies—but the bottom line is you can't play by the old rules. The old rules say to send everybody off to boot camp. The new rules say you can't do that anymore.

Roger Harrison:

I have this hope that there's a little window of opportunity that is going to last about as long as the people who were transformed during that opening up period in the 1970s. While those people are in their most productive years, while they are in positions of power and responsibility, I feel like there's a little window during which transformational change has the possibility of happening. It really depends on interactions between those people and what goes on in the world that hooks their idealism and makes it worthwhile for them to take the personal risk required to make things happen.

Stanford Janger is co-founder of The Close-Up Foundation *in Washington, D.C., and currently a consultant based in Santa Fe, New Mexico. He is a graduate of Harvard University.*

Amy Edmondson is director of research at Pecos River Learning Centers, Inc. in Santa Fe and the author of A Fuller Explanation: The Synergetic Geometry of R. Buckminster Fuller *(Birkhauser, 1987). She is a graduate of Harvard University.*

Afterword Notes

1. Semler (1989), 79.
2. Ibid., 76.
3. Ibid., 79.
4. Ibid.
5. Ibid., 84.
6. Killmann (1988), 1.
7. Ibid., xiii.
8. Sinetar (1987), 21.
9. Spencer (1989), 19.
10. Sinetar (1987), 21.
11. Ibid., 25.
12. Levering (1988), 49.
13. Chouinard (1989), 54.
14. Rutigliano (1986), 37.
15. Hawken (1989), 73.
16. Street (1988), 24.
17. Barnes (1988), 70.
18. Steinberg (1988), 52.
19. Pascarella (1989)
20. Harrison (1983), 216.
21. O'Toole (1985), 49.
22. Gussow (1989), 18.
23. O'Toole (1985), 342.
24. Ibid., 50.
25. Ibid., 291.
26. Semler (1989), 84.
27. Rhodes (1982), 34.
28. O'Toole (1985), 95.
29. Burlingham (1989), 50.
30. Hawken (1987), 169.
31. Burlingham (1989), 50.
32. Sinetar (1987), 25.
33. O'Toole (1985), 94.
34. Ibid., 85.
35. Ibid., 85.
36. Semler (1989), 82.
37. Rutigliano (1986), 37.
38. Hawken (1987), 214.
39. O'Toole (1985), 100.
40. Levering (1988), 49.
41. Kelley (1989), 54.
42. O'Toole (1985), 86.
43. Ibid., 133.
44. Ibid., 87.
45. Hawken (1987), 212.
46. Ibid., 214.
47. Ibid., 224.
48. O'Toole (1985), 129.
49. Rutigliano (1986), 37.
50. O'Toole (1985).
51. Ibid., 91.
52. Peters (1987), 4.
53. Hartman (1986), 38.
54. Hawken (1987), 198.
55. Peters (1989), 92.
56. Hawken (1989), 72.
57. Birch (1987), 7.
58. Hawken, (1989) 73.
59. Birch (1987), 17.
60. Tichy (1989), 114-5.
61. Hawken (1989), 72.
62. Interview with author.
63. Interview with author.
64. Adams (1988), 62.
65. Woodward (1987), xiv.
66. O'Toole (1985), 289.
67. Pascarella (1989), 4.
68. Kilmann (1988), 7.
69. Gauthier (1988-89) 5.
70. Kilmann (1988), 7.
71. Ibid., 190.
72. O'Toole (1985), 274.
73. Interview with author.
74. Tichy (1989), 120.
75. Clurman (1990), 4.
76. O'Toole (1985), 75.

Bibliography

The stage on which we cast our drama is so vast, and the scope of relevant subject matter is so extensive, that a comprehensive bibliography would be tedious and of little use. Instead, we have chosen to include a very selective choice of a few sources we have found particularly helpful. Most of the items listed below contain their own bibliographies, which can lead the interested reader to many more specific sources.

Adams, John & Sabina Spencer (1988), "People in Transition," *Training and Development Journal*, Oct. pp. 61-63.

Adams, John, ed. (1984), *Transforming Work*. Alexandria, VA: Miles River Press.

Adams, John ed. (1986), *Transforming Leadership*. Alexandria, VA: Miles River Press.

Angrist, Stanley W. (1983), "Classless Capitalists," *Forbes*, May 9, pp. 122-124.

Barnes, John (1988), "A Natural Formula For Success." *U.S. News & World Report*, Dec. 12.

Bateson, Gregory (1972), *Steps to an Ecology of Mind*. New York: Ballantine.

Berman, Morris (1981), *The Reënchantment of the World*. Ithaca, NY: Cornell University Press.

Berry, Thomas (1988), *The Dream of the Earth*. San Francisco: Sierra Club Books

Berry, Wendell (1978), *The Unsettling of America: Culture and Agriculture*, New York: Avon/Sierra Club Books.

Birch, David (1987), *Job Creation in America*. New York: Free Press.

Birke, Lynda (1986), *Women, Feminism, and Biology: The Feminist Challenge*. London: Harvester Press.

Bookchin, Murray (1978), "Toward a Liberatory Technology," in *Stepping Stones: Appropriate Technology and Beyond* (Lane de Moll and Gigi Coe, eds.). New York: Schocken Books.

Borsodi, Ralph (1948), *Education and Living*. Suffern, New York: The School of Living.

Boulding, Kenneth (1970), "Economics of the Coming Spaceship Earth," in *The Environmental Handbook*, ed. Garrett de Bell. New York: Ballantine.

Boulding, Kenneth (1978), *Ecodynamics: A New Theory of Societal Evolution*. London: Sage.

Brown, Lester R. (1981), *Building a Sustainable Society*. New York: W. W. Norton.

Brown, Lester R. (1988), *State of the World, 1988: A Worldwatch Institute Report on Progress Toward a Sustainable Society*. New York: Norton. (Similar publications every year since 1984.)

Burlingham, Bo (1989), "Being the Boss," *Inc. Magazine*, Oct. pp. 49-65.

Capra, Fritjof (1982), *The Turning Point: Science, Society, and the Rising Culture*. New York: Bantam.

Carson, Rachel (1962), *Silent Spring*. Cambridge, MA: Riverside Press.

Chouinard, Yvon (1988), "Coming of Age—Yvon Chouinard," *Inc. Magazine*, Apr.

Clark, Mary (1989), *Ariadne's Thread: The Search for New Modes of Thinking*. New York: St. Martin's Press.

Clurman, Carol (1990), "More Than Just a Paycheck," *USA Weekend*, Jan. 19-21 pp. 4-5.

Commoner, Barry (1971), *The Closing Circle: Nature, Man, and Technology*. New York: Alfred A. Knopf.

Congdon, R. J., ed. (1977), *Introduction to Appropriate Technology: Toward a Simpler Lifestyle*. Emmaus, PA: Rodale Press.

Daly, Herman (1977), *Steady-State Economics: The Economics of Biophysical Equilibrium and Moral Growth*. San Francisco: W. H. Freeman.

Daly, Herman, and John B. Cobb (1989), *For the Common Good: Rededicating the Economy Toward Community, the Environment, and a Sustainable Future*. Boston: Beacon Press.

Davies, James C. (1971), *When Men Rebel and Why*. New York: Free Press.

Davis, W. Jackson (1979), *The Seventh Year: Industrial Civilization in Transition*. New York: W. W. Norton.

De Pree, Max (1989), *Leadership is an Art*. New York: Doubleday

Devall, Bill, and George Sessions (1985), *Deep Ecology: Living as if Nature Mattered*. Salt Lake City: Peregrine Smith Books.

Eisler, Riane (1987), *The Chalice and the Blade: Our History, Our Future*. New York: Harper & Row.

Elgin, Duane (1981), *Voluntary Simplicity: Toward a Way of Life That is Outwardly Simple, Inwardly Rich*. New York: William Morrow & Co.

Ellul, Jacques (1964), *The Technological Society*. (Original French edition 1954) New York: Vintage/Random House.

Ferguson, Marilyn (1980), *The Aquarian Conspiracy: Personal and Social Transformation in the 1980s*. Los Angeles: Jeremy Tarcher.

Fox, Matthew (1983), *Original Blessing: A Primer in Creation Spirituality*. Santa Fe: Bear & Co.

Gauthier, Thomas D. (1988/89), "The Improvement Practitioner: Agent for Change." *National Productivity Review*, vol. 8 no. 1 pp. 5-10.

Gussow, Alan (1989), "Green Consumerism," *In Business*, Nov/Dec. pp. 18-9.

Harman, Willis (1988), *Global Mind Change*. Indianapolis: Knowledge Systems.

Harman, Willis, "The Need for a Restructuring of Science." *ReVision* vol. 11 no. 2, Fall 1988 pp. 13-21.

Harrison, Roger (1983), "Strategies for a New Age," *Human Resource Management*, vol. 22 no. 3 pp. 209-235.

Hartman, Curtis (1986), "Values Added," *Inc. Magazine*, Jan. pp. 29-39.

Hawken, Paul (1987), *Growing a Business*. New York: Fireside.

Hawken, Paul (1989), "Entrepreneurs: The Real Cultural Revolutionaries," *Utne Reader*, no. 31 Jan/Feb. pp. 72-73.

Heilbroner, Robert (1980), *An Inquiry Into the Human Prospect*. Revised ed. New York: Norton.

Henderson, Hazel (1988), *The Politics of the Solar Age: Alternatives to Economics.* Indianapolis: Knowledge Systems.

Hutchins, Robert M. (1968), *The Learning Society.* New York: Praeger.

Kelly, Marjorie (1989), "Revolution in the Marketplace," *Utne Reader,* no. 31 Jan/Feb. pp. 54-62.

Kilmann, Ralph H. (1988), Teresa Joyce Covin, and Associates, *Corporate Transformation.* San Francisco: Jossey-Bass.

King, Ursula (1989), *Women and Spirituality: Voices of Protest and Promise.* New York: Macmillan Education.

Klinkenborg, Verlyn (1988), "Adventures of a Renaissance Fun Hog," *Esquire,* Jan. pp. 92-98.

Koestler, Arthur (1984), *The Invisible Writing.* Briarcliff Manor, NY: Stein and Day.

Kohr, Leopold (1978), *The Overdeveloped Nations: The Diseconomies of Scale.* (Original edition in 1962, in Spanish and German) New York: Schocken Books.

Land, George, and Beth Jarman (1989), *Breakpoint and Beyond,* unpub. ms.

Leopold, Aldo (1966), *A Sand County Almanac.* New York: Ballantine.

Lerner, Gerda (1985), *The Creation of Patriarchy.* New York: Oxford University Press.

Levering, Robert (1988), "Paradise, Corporate-Style," *Business Month,* Jul/Aug. pp. 47-50.

Lovelock, J. E. (1979), *Gaia: A New Look at Life on Earth.* New York: Oxford University Press.

Lutz, Mark A. and Kenneth Lux (1979), *The Challenge of Humanistic Economics.* Menlo Park, CA: Benjamin/Cummings.

Maccoby, Michael (1988), *Why Work: Leading the New Generation.* New York: Simon and Schuster.

Macy, Joanna (1983), *Despair and Personal Power in the Nuclear Age.* Philadelphia: New Society Publishers.

Macy, Joanna, et al. (1989), *Thinking Like a Mountain: Toward a Council of All Beings.* Philadelphia: New Society Publishers.

Meeks, Fleming (1989), "The Man Is The Message," *Forbes,* Apr. 17 pp. 148-152.

Merchant, Carolyn (1980), *The Death of Nature: Women, Ecology, and the Scientific Revolution.* New York: Harper & Row.

Mollner, Terry (1990), *Mondragon: The Journey From the Material Age to the Relationship Age Has Begun.* New York: Doubleday.

Muller, Robert (1982), *New Genesis: Shaping a Global Spirituality.* New York: Doubleday & Co.

Mumford, Lewis (1956), *The Transformations of Man.* New York: Harper and Brothers.

Murray, Bertram (1974), "What the Ecologists Can Teach the Economists," in Susan Mehrtens and Charles Jezek, eds., *Earthkeeping: Readings in Human Ecology.* Pacific Grove, CA: Boxwood Press.

Myers, Norman (1984), *GAIA: An Atlas of Planet Management.* New York: Anchor Books.

Naisbitt, John, and Patricia Aburdene (1985), *Re-inventing the Corporation.* New York: Warner.

O'Toole, James (1985), *Vanguard Management.* New York: Doubleday & Co.

Ornstein, Robert, and Paul Ehrlich (1989), *New World, New Mind.* New York: Doubleday.

Pascarella, Perry (1984), *The New Achievers.* New York: Free Press.

Pascarella, Perry and Mark A. Frohman (1989), *The Purpose Driven Organization.* San Francisco: Jossey-Bass.

Peters, Thomas J. (1987), *Thriving on Chaos.* New York: Alfred A. Knopf.

Peters, Thomas J. (1989), "Doubting Thomas," *Inc. Magazine,* Apr. pp. 82-92.

Popper, Karl R. and John C. Eccles (1981), *The Self and Its Brain.* Springer International.

Rhodes, Lucien (1982), "The Un-Manager," *Inc. Magazine,* Aug. pp. 34-46.

Robertson, James (1979), *The Sane Alternative: A Choice of Futures.* St. Paul, MN: River Basin Publishing.

Robertson, James (1990), *Future Wealth: A New Economics for the 21st Century.* England: Cassell Publishers Inc.

Rossner, John (1989), *In Search of the Primordial Tradition.* St. Paul, MN: Llewellyn Publications.

Roszak, Theodore (1978), *Person/Planet: The Creative Disintegration of Industrial Society.* Garden City, NY: Doubleday.

Ruether, Rosemary R. (1975), *New Woman, New Earth: Sexist Ideologies and Human Liberation.* New York: Seabury Press.

Rutigliano, Anthony J. (1986), "Some Would Call It Paternalism," *Management Review,* Jul. pp. 34-37.

Sale, Kirkpatrick (1980), *Human Scale.* New York: Coward, McCann and Geoghegan.

Satin, Mark (1979), *New Age Politics: Healing Self and Society.* New York: Delta.

Schaef, Anne Wilson (1987), *When Society Becomes an Addict.* New York: Harper & Row.

Schumacher, E.F. (1973), *Small is Beautiful: Economics as if People Mattered.* New York: Harper & Row.

Schumacher, E.F. (1979), *Good Work.* New York: Harper Colophon.

Semler, Ricardo (1989), "Managing Without Managers." *Harvard Business Review,* vol. 67 no. 5 pp. 76-84.

Senge, Peter M. (1986), "The New Management: Moving From Invention to Innovation," *New Management* pp. 7-13.

Sinetar, Marsha (1987), "The Actualized Worker," *Futurist,* Mar/Apr. pp. 21-25.

Snow, C.P. (1959), *The Two Cultures and the Scientific Revolution.* New York: Cambridge University Press.

Sorokin, Pitirim (1941), *Social and Cultural Dynamics.* New Brunswick, NJ: Transaction Publishing.

Sorokin, Pitirim (1954), *The Ways and Power of Love.* Boston: Beacon Press.

Spencer, Sabina (1989), "Purpose and Spirit," *Organizational Development Practitioner,* June. pp. 18-20.

Sperry, Roger (1987), "Structure and Significance of the Consciousness Revolution." *Jour. Mind and Behavior* vol. 8 no. 1 pp. 37-66.

Sperry, Roger (1981), "Changing Priorities." *Annual Review of Neurosciences* (1981) pp.1-10.

Spretnak, Charlene and Fritjof Capra (1986), *Green Politics*. Santa Fe, NM: Bear and Co.

Spretnak, Charlene, ed. (1982), *The Politics of Women's Spirituality*. New York: Anchor/Doubleday.

Steinberg, Jon (1988), "The Body Biz." *Ms.*, Sept. pp. 50-53.

Street, Red (1988), "Campaign in a Jar." *American Health*, Dec. 88.

Tart, Charles, ed., (1975), *Transpersonal Psychologies*. New York: Harper & Row.

Theobald, Robert (1987), *The Rapids of Change: Social Entrepreneurship in Turbulent Times*. Indianapolis: Knowledge Systems.

Tichy, Noel and Ram Charan (1989), "Speed, Simplicity, Self-Confidence: An Interview with Jack Welch." *Harvard Business Review*, vol. 67 no. 5, pp. 112-120.

Toffler, Alvin (1981), *The Third Wave*. New York: Bantam.

Vaughan, Frances and Roger Walsh (1980), *Beyond Ego: Transpersonal Dimensions in Psychology*. Los Angeles: J.P. Tarcher.

Veltrop, Bill and Karin Harrington (1988), "Roadmap to New Organizational Territory," *Training and Development Journal*, June.

Wald, George (1988), "The Cosmology of Life and Mind," in *Synthesis of Science and Religion: Critical Essays and Dialogues*. San Francisco: Bhaktivedanta Institute.

White, Mary and Dorothy Van Soest (1984), *Empowerment of People for Peace*. Minneapolis: Women Against Military Madness.

Wilber, Ken (1983), *Eye to Eye*. New York: Anchor Books.

Winner, Langdon (1977), *Autonomous Technology. Cambridge:* MIT Press.

Woodward, Harry and Steve Buchholz (1987), *Aftershock: Helping People Through Corporate Change*. New York: John Wiley & Sons.

World Commission on Environment and Development (The Brundtland Commission) (1987), *Our Common Future*. New York: Oxford University Press.

Zuboff, Shoshanna (1988), *In the Age of the Smart Machine: The Future of Work and Power*. New York: Basic Books.

About the Authors

Willis Harman

Willis Harman's life spans two World Wars and one Cold War, and comprises three careers. Following service as a naval officer in World War II, he taught electrical engineering and engineering systems at the University of Florida and Stanford University, and published several textbooks. Then for 16 years he was on the staff of Stanford Research Institute (now SRI International), involved with futures research and strategic planning. That work is summarized in *An Incomplete Guide to the Future* (W. W. Norton, 1979) and *Changing Images of Man* (co-authored with O. W. Markley; Pergamon, 1980). In 1978 he moved to his present position, as president of the Institute of Noetic Sciences, involved with the challenge to the sciences represented by the many facets and capacities of human consciousness.

In the early 1970s, while engaged in research on the future for a variety of business and government clients, Willis became impressed with the indications that Western industrial society is approaching a transformational watershed comparable to the transition from medieval to modern times. He began to interpret both the problems of modern society and the rise of new social movements in this broad context. Finally, convinced that the most important change taking place in modern society is at the deepest level of underlying assumptions about the nature of ourselves and the universe in which we live, he joined the Institute of Noetic Sciences to be able to devote more of his time and efforts to understanding that shift and its implications. This work is summarized in two books, *Higher Creativity* (co-authored with Howard Rheingold; Tarcher, 1984) and *Global Mind Change* (Knowledge Systems, 1988).

In the late 1980s, Willis joined with a group of businesspersons to form the World Business Academy, an association of business executives with a common commitment to establishing a positive role for business in the creation of a better world future.

John Hormann

John Hormann's absorbing concern is "well-being for us and our planet through communication and world trade." To him, this is a possible goal once we dissolve the conflicts of opposing forces (dualities) which we create through our own "causality thinking."

"Causality thinking" is an effective concept for studying the structures of reality. Indeed, it is the usual way of thinking in Western science. However, as John sees it, our concentration on practicability and repeatability has narrowed our perception of reality and has conditioned us to be one-track goal seekers, to be both time driven and judgmental.

Causality thinking turns dangerous, in John's view, where it is absolutely set as the method for cognizing reality and mastering life. It binds our minds to its own constructions and we become unaware of higher possibilities, negating that part of reality which is not "measurable."

John Hormann was educated in Germany and in the U.S. He has worked over 25 years for IBM in various international management positions. Presently he is on a three-year assignment to the Schweisfurth Foundation in Munich.

The Institute of Noetic Sciences

Astronaut Edgar Mitchell founded this nonprofit membership organization in 1973 to expand knowledge of the nature and potentials of the mind and spirit, and to apply that knowledge to advance health and well-being for humankind and our planet. He chose the word *noetic*—from the Greek "nous," meaning mind, intelligence and understanding. The "noetic sciences," then, are those that *encompass diverse ways of knowing:* the reasoning processes of the intellect, the perceptions of the physical senses, and the intuitive, spiritual, inner ways of knowing.

The Institute funds scientific research; brings top-level scientists and scholars together to share their methods, perspectives and knowledge; and, in publications to its members, discusses new developments in consciousness research.

Emerging Paradigms in Science and Society Program

This Institute Program explores the relationship between consciousness—particularly values and beliefs—and global issues, and the premise that *a fundamental change of mind* may be occurring worldwide, for example, in areas such as global peace and common security. In its newest project, "Expanding the Foundations of Science," the Institute is attempting to identify and illuminate the changing *foundations* of science—evident in the exciting new developments in physics, biology, the neurosciences, systems theory and other fields. These developments provide startling insights into understanding the basic processes of health and healing, psychology, parapsychology, sociology and international relations. In fact, the Institute believes these changes in the very foundations of science will generate a "global mind change" every bit as sweeping as the dramatic change in worldview accompanying the scientific revolution in the seventeenth century.

In this context, the Emerging Paradigms Program explores the role of business in a positive global future. More and more business leaders are realizing their corporate "mission" is much greater than profits—it includes people development, education, and helping solve the "global problematique." To help foster this "mind shift" in business, the Institute works with an international network of visionary executives and entrepreneurs to explore the role of intuitive leadership in business, advance adult learning and creativity, and employ corporate resources to create a positive global future. *Creative Work: The Constructive Role of Business in a Transforming Society* arises directly out of Willis Harman's and John Hormann's research and experience in this exciting and promising new field.

The Inner Mechanisms of the Healing Response Program

One of the fundamental goals of the Institute has been to create a scientific understanding of the mind-body relationship. The Institute's Inner Mechanisms Program is devoted to studying *how* the healing response functions. This Program asks: What are the innate processes within us that stimulate recovery and natural self-repair? Is there an unknown healing system that promotes remission from normally fatal illnesses? The Institute supports proposals from selected researchers and targeted interdisciplinary working conferences on the mechanisms of healing, in areas such as psychoneuroimmunology, energy medicine, spontaneous remission and spiritual healing.

The Exceptional Abilities Program

The Institute seeks to foster a vital, contemporary vision of constructive human potentials—a vision that incorporates all that is known about the farther and higher reaches of human nature. By studying people with outstanding and extraordinary capacities, such as exceptional creativity, physical performance or mental ability, the Institute hopes to learn how individuals can better realize and expand their unique abilities—and, with them, create a world that supports human fulfillment.

The Altruistic Spirit Program

In the Altruistic Spirit Program the Institute studies the human capacity for unselfish love and creatively altruistic behavior. The Institute hopes to discover the conditions that foster or suppress creative altruism, and encourage its presence in everyday life.

The Institute's pioneering research and educational programs are financed completely by donations from members and other sources of private support.

Institute members receive a quarterly journal, the *Noetic Sciences Review*, which offers serious discussion of emerging concepts in consciousness research, the mind-body connection and healing, and our changing global reality. Members also receive occasional *Special Reports*, which provide a deeper look into specific issues within these areas; the quarterly *Noetic Sciences Bulletin*, with reports on continuing Institute projects, member activities, and upcoming conferences and lectures; and *An Intelligent Guide*, a comprehensive catalog of the many books, audiotapes and videotapes in this field, which are available to members at a discount.

The Institute of Noetic Sciences
475 Gate Five Road, Suite 300
Sausalito, California 94965-0909
(415) 331-5650

Index